THE

Essential 55

WORKBOOK

Also by Ron Clark

The Essential 55

The Excellent 11

THE
Essential 55

WORKBOOK

Ron Clark

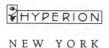

HYPERION

NEW YORK

Library of Congress Cataloging-in-Publication Data

Clark, Ron
   The essential 55 workbook / Ron Clark.
      p. cm.
   ISBN 1-4013-0770-1 (alk. paper)
   1. Teaching. 2. Conduct of life. I. Title: Essential fifty-five workbook. II. Clark, Ron,
—Essential 55. III. Title.

LB1025.3.C5343 2004
371.102—dc22

                                                                    2004042448

Hyperion books are available for special promotions and premiums. For details contact Michael Rentas, Manager, Inventory and Premium Sales, Hyperion, 77 West 66th Street, 11th floor, New York, New York 10023-6298, or call 212-456-0133.

FIRST EDITION

10   9   8   7   6   5   4   3   2   1

Dear Parents,

I was seven years old and it was a typical day after school. I was preparing to eat an orange and begin my homework as I watched Guiding Light *with my father and grandmother. I was really into the show at the moment, because I think Roger Thorpe had kidnapped his wife and their daughter. The wife's ex-boyfriend Bob Bauer was planning her escape from the caves of some mountain. I watched, spellbound, as I clumsily peeled the orange. Suddenly I noticed that I didn't have a paper towel or anywhere to put the peelings, and I certainly didn't want to get up and miss the show. I took a quick glance at my father, entranced in the show, and a quick glance at my grandmother, snoring, and I knew I was home free. I imitated a yawn and quickly tossed a handful of peelings behind the couch. Suddenly Roger Thorpe was dangling from a bridge; his only hope was Bob Bauer, his arch-enemy, who was clutching his hands. Would he save him? Would he let him drop? Another handful of peelings behind the couch. Suddenly there was a Bounty commercial, appropriately enough, and my father asked, "Ron, are you enjoying that orange?" I responded, "Yes sir, it's really good." My father smiled and then asked, "Ron, where are you putting the peelings?" Without hesitation and with the most convincing of looks on my face I said, "I'm eating them." My father just said okay and we went back to watching the show. I remember giggling inside as I finished the orange and threw the rest of the peelings behind the couch. When the show was over my father asked, "Ron, would you help me do something?" "Sure," I responded. He then asked me to help him move the couch. My eyes were wide as saucers, but I couldn't act guilty. I jumped up and as we moved the couch all of the peelings were revealed. "Where do you think these came from?" he asked, and I just said, "Mudder (my sleeping grandmother) probably did it." Okay, I was desperate.*

I was punished that day, and I will never forget the words my father said to me. He asked if I knew why I was being punished, and I said it was because I threw the peelings behind the couch. He let me know that my punishment had nothing to do with the peelings. He said I was being punished because I had lied to him and in doing so I had disrespected him.

As I grew up, I received many talks like that. Everyone in my family, from my grandmother, to my parents, to my aunts and uncles, raised me in a way that placed an emphasis on respecting others, having manners, and being honest. I had a true Southern upbringing, and I am so thankful to have been surrounded with so much love, wisdom, and respect. One of the keys of the process, however, deals with patience. Taking the time to talk with kids, like my father did that day, is crucial. We need to explain, step by step, what we expect from children, but more importantly, we have to make sure they understand why it's important to have manners and respect. I have found that once that is accomplished, children will begin to make great efforts to do as we have asked.

When I first started teaching, there were so many discipline problems that I couldn't even get the students' attention. I tried everything I could think of, and then I decided to do something different. I had always heard a teacher should have no more than five general rules for his or her students, but I decided to try and be more specific and spell out exactly what I expected of my students and give them examples of how they should act in all situations. I just made a simple list of expectations for them, but it soon grew to a list of "55 Essentials." On the first day of school, I took the time to discuss each one with my students and let them know its importance. We would then role-play each rule and practice it over and over. Throughout the year, the rules were reminded, enforced, and encouraged. Every year I was amazed at how it really worked as I watched my students develop manners, respect, and self-esteem and as I saw their test scores go through the roof. My list of "55 Essentials" seemed so simple and obvious, but it provided my students with a guideline that showed them exactly how they could become better students and better people.

This past year, it has been great to hear of so many teachers who are using the 55 rules in their classrooms, but it has been especially wonderful to hear from parents who are using the rules at home, reading one rule each night to their kids at bedtime, implementing the rules during dinner, and taking the time to teach the manners that I learned when I was growing up. To hear parents who are appreciative of having the 55 rules listed in a manner that they can use has been exciting and humbling. Some parents who read The Essential 55 have asked that I provide them with some type of book that would show them activities and tips they could use with their children that would help teach and enforce the manners, and from that request this workbook was born. I hope it meets the expectations of the parents who use it, and I also hope it is approved by the toughest critics ever, their children!

I tell my students all the time, a person can have the best education in the world, but it will mean nothing if that person doesn't treat others with kindness, have respect for the individuals he or she comes in contact with, and attempt to use the knowledge and skills they have obtained to help others. I would rather have a son who was full of compassion than a son with a perfect SAT score. That is not even a contest. What we are aiming for, however, and what I hope this workbook will do is to help us all raise students who are not only brilliant but who are also respectful, well-mannered, and dedicated to making a difference in the lives of others. That is the key not only to raising kids, but also to improving our communities and the state of education in America.

As a teacher, I would like to thank every parent who intends to use this book in their home. Sending your children to school with manners and respect is the number one thing I would ask of any parent. That makes the job of the teacher so much easier and more enjoyable. Your concern for raising your children in the best possible way is a beautiful thing, and I wish you all the best as you deal with the challenges all children present, those difficult decisions you'll have to make, and your own types of misplaced orange peelings. Good luck along the journey of helping your child be the best he or she can possibly be. Thank you!

—Ron Clark

RULE #1

When responding to any adult, your child must answer by saying, "Yes, ma'am" or "No, sir." It is not acceptable to just nod one's head or say only yes or no.

Activity #1

Does your child think she knows how to talk to adults? Give her this quiz to find out. Encourage her to answer truthfully, and circle her answers. Then add up the numbers assigned to each answer and find her score. Discuss the score with your child. Help her figure out why another response might be more appropriate.

1. "Is there a reason why you are late for class?" said Mrs. Jones, the math teacher.

   KID A: "Yes, my locker was stuck. Sorry." (2)
   KID B: "I guess so." (1)
   KID C: "Yes, ma'am. I couldn't open my locker. I'm really sorry." (3)

2. "You wanted to see me?" asked Miss Carlson, the guidance counselor.

   KID A: "Yes. Can you help me figure out what to do after
   graduation?" (2)

KID B: "Yes, ma'am. I was hoping you could help me make plans for after graduation." (3)

KID C: "Yeah. What can you do for me?" (1)

3. "I need help getting your baby brother ready for day care," said Stan's mom. "Can you give me a hand?"

KID A: "If I have to." (1)

KID B: "Sure, Mom. In a minute." (2)

KID C: "Of course, Mom. What do you need?" (3)

4. "Could you tell me why you'd like to work at the record store?" asked Mr. Drew during a job interview.

KID A: "Well, sir, I think your store is really great, and I know a lot about music." (3)

KID B: "Well, it would be really cool. A lot of my friends shop here." (1)

KID C: "This place is the best! You play the best music!" (2)

5. (from the same interview) "Thank you. We'll be in touch," Mr. Drew said, shaking the teen's hand.

KID A: "Great! Talk to you soon!" (2)

KID B: "Thank you, sir. It was nice meeting you." (3)

KID C: "Do you think I have the job?" (1)

6. "Hello, Janet! I hope you enjoyed the book your grandmother and I gave you for your birthday," said Janet's grandfather.

KID A: "No, sir. I haven't had a chance to read it. But thanks so much!" (3)

KID B: "Nope. No time. See ya!" (1)

KID C: "No, it's still sitting on my shelf. It looks interesting, though." (2)

7. "I'm glad you came to visit, Max," said Aunt Helen.

KID A: "It was fun. Thanks!" (2)
KID B: "You have a great house, Aunt Helen. Thanks for inviting me." (3)
KID C: "Sure, no problem." (1)

8. "Can I help you?" asked the woman who worked at the shoe store.

KID A: "No." (2)
KID B: "We'll call you when we need you." (1)
KID C: "No, thank you. We're just browsing." (3)

9. "Could someone please explain to me why you need to make so much noise?" said Mrs. Myers, the next-door neighbor.

KID A: "We're sorry, ma'am. We'll try to keep it down." (3)
KID B: "Sorry. We'll turn down the music." (2)
KID C: "If you don't like it, too bad." (1)

10. "Can I help you?" asked the media specialist at the library.

KID A: "Yeah. I need a video on volcanoes." (1)
KID B: "Yes, sir. I'm looking for a video on volcanoes. Can you help
me?" (3)
KID C: "Yes! I'm looking for volcano videos. Do you have
any?" (2)

25–30: Good job! You're usually very polite to adults. You know when to say "sir" or "ma'am," and you speak to adults with respect.

17–24: Not bad! You could still use some work, though, in being polite and respectful. Try to throw in a few more "sirs" and "ma'ams."

10–16: You need some work when you talk to adults. Your responses are abrupt and impolite. Try to think about how you would like adults to talk to you. They'll be more respectful if you are more respectful of them.

Activity #2

Now it's time to role-play! Each scenario below is a miniplay, with only six lines each. Invite your child to read the part of the "kid" while you speak the adult roles. After each scenario, talk about how the kid's response might be considered disrespectful or impolite to an adult. Then help your child to write new dialogue for the kid, perhaps adding a few "sirs" or "ma'ams." Read the new play out loud with your child, comparing the tone of the dialogue with the original dialogue.

SCENARIO #1

GRANDFATHER: Hi, Tim! How is school going?

KID: Fine.

GRANDFATHER: Do you have any classes that you like this year?

KID: Biology is okay, I guess.

GRANDFATHER: Really! I used to like biology, too. What's your favorite part about it?

KID: Um, don't know. Plant stuff, I guess.

NOW IT'S YOUR TURN:

GRANDFATHER: Hi, Tim! How is school going?

KID: _____

GRANDFATHER: Do you have any classes that you like this year?

KID: _____

GRANDFATHER: Really! I used to like biology, too. What's your favorite
part about it?

KID: _____

SCENARIO #2

MR. TURNER, TEACHER: Thanks for meeting with me, Tom. I wanted to
talk about your schoolwork. It seems to be slipping a bit lately.
KID: Sorry I've been busy with the soccer team.
MR. TURNER: Is soccer getting in the way of your schoolwork?
KID: No, man. I mean, I know I have to do my homework and stuff.
MR. TURNER: Would you like me to help you after school?
KID: Okay, if you think it will help.

NOW IT'S YOUR TURN:

MR. TURNER, TEACHER: Thanks for meeting with me, Tom. I wanted to
talk about your schoolwork. It seems to be slipping a bit lately.

KID: _____

MR. TURNER: Is soccer getting in the way of your schoolwork?

KID: _____

MR. TURNER: Would you like me to help you after school?

KID: _____

SCENARIO #3

MRS. FLETCHER, PRINCIPAL: What are you doing in the hallway?
    Shouldn't you be in class?
KID: Uh, yeah.
MRS. FLETCHER: Does your teacher know that you're out here?
KID: Yeah, he sent me to get some mural paper.
MRS. FLETCHER: Mural paper is hard to carry by yourself. Do you need
    some help?
KID: Uh, no. I got it.

NOW IT'S YOUR TURN:

MRS. FLETCHER, PRINCIPAL: What are you doing in the hallway?
    Shouldn't you be in class?

KID: _____

MRS. FLETCHER: Does your teacher know that you're out here?

KID: _____

MRS. FLETCHER: Mural paper is hard to carry by yourself. Do you need some help?

KID: _____

SCENARIO #4

MRS. WILLIAMS, STORE MANAGER: I could really use some extra help on Saturday during the sale. Do you think you could come in a few minutes early?
KID: Sure, if you really need me to.
MRS. WILLIAMS: That would be great! Would half an hour be okay?
KID: I don't know. I need to check with my parents.
MRS. WILLIAMS: Thanks, Melissa. That would help me a lot.
KID: Uh-huh.

NOW IT'S YOUR TURN:

MRS. WILLIAMS, STORE MANAGER: I could really use some extra help on Saturday during the sale. Do you think you could come in a few minutes early?

KID: _____
MRS. WILLIAMS: That would be great! Would half an hour be okay?

KID: _____
MRS. WILLIAMS: Thanks, Melissa. That would help me a lot.

KID: _____

RULE #2

Teach your child the value of eye contact. When someone is speaking, your child should keep his eyes on the person at all times. If someone else makes a comment, your child should turn and face that person.

Activity #1

When speaking to friends, family members, teachers, and people in the community, does your child look the person in the eye, or does he look around, at the floor, anywhere but at the person? Present this quiz to your child, and have him place a check in the correct column to honestly show how he talks to people. You might want to complete the quiz yourself and compare your responses with his. Then you both can try the activities on pages 9–12 to improve your eye-contact expertise.

———

	MAKE EYE CONTACT	DO NOT MAKE EYE CONTACT
1. You meet a friend on the street. You . . .	_____	_____
2. You meet an older relative. You . . .	_____	_____
3. You give the cashier at the store money for your purchases. You . . .	_____	_____
4. You take your lunch tray from the person working in the cafeteria. You . . .	_____	_____
5. Your teacher asks you a question. You . . .	_____	_____
6. You explain to your parents or boss why you didn't finish your chores or an assignment. You . . .	_____	_____
7. You ask permission to go to a special function. You . . .	_____	_____
8. You tell your teacher or boss that you you would like to volunteer for some extra-credit work. You . . .	_____	_____

	MAKE EYE CONTACT	DO NOT MAKE EYE CONTACT
9. You explain to a friend why you can't hang out after school. You . . .	_____	_____
10. You tell guests at your party that you're really glad they could come. You . . .	_____	_____

Activity #2

Look at the checks your child has made in the "Do Not Make Eye Contact" column. Find each scenario below. Then work with him to practice making eye contact as you both ad-lib each situation. Choose your own troublesome scenarios, and ask for his advice, too.

A. You meet a friend in the street.

Play the role of your child's friend, and begin an impromptu conversation. Be sure to look your child in the eye, encouraging him to meet your eyes, as well.

B. You meet an older relative.

Pretend to be an older relative in your family, such as a grandparent, aunt, uncle, or older cousin. Begin a typical conversation between your child and the older relative, asking such questions as "What grade are you in now?" and "How do you like school?" Each time your child answers, be sure she makes eye contact. If not, lean down to meet her eyes halfway.

C. You give the cashier at the store money for your purchases.

For this scenario, let your child take the role of the cashier as you play the role of the customer, not meeting the cashier's eyes. Afterward, ask him how it felt to have the "customer" not make eye contact. For example, did he as the cashier feel uncomfortable or even insulted? Replay the scene, this time making eye contact, and have your child analyze the difference that eye contact can make in how he feels.

D. You take your lunch tray from the person working in the school cafeteria.

Let your child take the role of the cafeteria worker while you take the role of the student. Keep your eyes downcast as you grab the "tray." (You might use a plate or platter from your kitchen to aid in the role-play.) Ask your child how she felt as you took the lunch tray. Then switch roles, and have her practice taking the tray from you and saying, "Thank you," making direct eye contact.

E. Your teacher asks you a question.

Set the stage in your home to resemble a mock classroom, perhaps using the kitchen table as the teacher's desk. You play the teacher sitting behind the table. Ask your child to approach you; then ask him a simple question. Tell him to react honestly—either making eye contact or not making eye contact. Practice the scenario several times, each time challenging him to keep his eyes focused on yours.

F. You explain to your parents or boss why you didn't finish your chores or an assignment.

Invite your child to "have the power" in this situation by being the parent or boss while you take the child's or employee's role. As you provide your explanation, look at the floor, scuff your toes, wiggle your hands, and so on. Then ask your child how she perceived you. Did she take your explanation seriously? Did your explanation sound sincere? Reverse roles, asking her to show *you* how *you* should have responded, complete with engaging eye contact.

G. You ask permission to go to a special function.

Suggest that your child wishes to go to a party or a concert but fears that you might object. Have him ask permission of you. Comment on his display of (or lack of) eye contact. Point out that the more eye contact he is able to make with you, the more seriously you would consider granting permission. Let him practice asking for permission and making eye contact as you ad-lib arriving at a decision.

H. You tell your teacher or boss that you would like to volunteer for some extra-credit work.

Tell your child that you are about to volunteer for a special project at work. Explain that you would like her to pretend to be your boss. Then begin to speak, occasionally making eye contact, but not always. Ask her if your query was successful; then try it again with more eye contact. Ask her which attempt was more effective, and talk about how making eye contact helps you connect with your boss—and helps your child connect with her teacher. Then let her try it as you reverse roles.

I. You explain to a friend why you can't hang out after school.

Encourage your child to act naturally while showing how he would tell a friend that he can't do something after school. Compliment him on his interpersonal skills; then suggest that he make more eye contact. Demonstrate how more eye contact makes his role in the conversation more sincere. Then invite him to try it again.

J. You tell guests at your party that you're really glad they could come.

Invite your child to be a "guest" at your party. Explain that the party is over and you are wishing your guests thanks and farewell. As you speak to your guest, do not make eye contact. You might take the role-play so far as to escort your child through a doorway. Then ask her if she believed that you were truly glad that she had come to the party. Repeat the exercise, this time making eye contact. Talk with your child about how a little thing like eye contact gives a thank-you a whole new meaning.

RULE #3

If someone in the class wins a game or does something well, your child should congratulate that person. Clapping should last at least three seconds, with the palms of both hands meeting in a manner that will give the appropriate clap volume.

Activity #1

Help your child recognize that offering congratulations for both big and small moments can make others feel great. Have him read each scenario on the next page and then fill in the blank lines with one of the words surrounded by confetti below. Tell him to write the numbered letters on the lines below to solve the mystery word. (Hint: Solving the word will also help him fill in all the words correctly!)

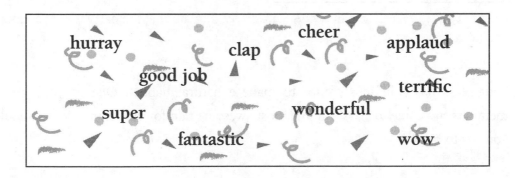

Your best friend won first place in the science fair. What should you say to her?

____ ____ ____ ____ ____ ____ ____ ____!
                                                   1

Your little brother received his first gold star in kindergarten. What should you say to him?

____ ____ ____ ____ ____!
11

One of your classmates got an A on a math test—for the very first time! What should you do?

____ ____ ____ ____!
       9

Your cousin passed the test to get her driver's license. What should you do?

____ ____ ____ ____ ____!
          5

Your class has split into groups to make a natural habitat. One of your group members has come to class with the most awesome rain forest diorama. What should you say to him?

____ ____ ____ ____ ____ ____ ____!
 4

Lots of kids on your soccer team can play really well, but one kid always sits on the bench. The coach finally calls her in to play a game. What should you say to her?

____ ____ ____ ____ ____ ____!
       8

Even though you really wanted the lead role in the school play, another kid in your class got the role instead. What should you do?

____ ____ ____ ____ ____ ____ ____!
           6

Your teacher has announced that one of the kids in your class has received a special award for perfect attendance. What should you say to him?

____ ____ ____ ____ ____ ____ ____ ____!
       7   10

Your older sister is written up in the newspaper for saving a litter of puppies during a rainstorm. What should you say to her?

____ ____ ____!
   2

The music teacher has chosen the best singers to perform at the holiday concert, but you were not one of them. What should you say to your singing classmates?

_____ _____ _____ _____ _____ _____ _____ _____ _____!
       3

Read this ryhme:

   It may be big.

   It may be small.

   But saying this word

   Covers it all:

Write the numbered letters on the lines below to solve the mystery word.

___ ___ ___ ___ ___ ___ ___ ___ ___ ___ ___ ___ ___ ___ ___!
1   2   3   4   5   6   7   8   9   6   7   10 2   3   11

Activity #2

When people announce the achievements of others, they sometimes give a short speech. And sometimes when people receive a special honor, like an award, they give a speech in return. Invite your child to write speeches for both situations. The next time he does something to make you proud, have him write a speech describing the achievement. Then, to accept the congratulations of others, ask him to write a speech to say "Thank you!" Encourage him to have fun reading the speech to you or to other members of the family. Use the speech starters on page 17 as a guide.

A SPECIAL ANNOUNCEMENT!

_____ has accomplished something terrific. _____

has _____

_____.

For _____'s special accomplishment, we would like to offer our

congratulations. Let's give _____ a round of applause! Con-

gratulations!

THANK YOU, THANK YOU, THANK YOU!

   Thank you so much for your congratulations! I felt as if I accomplished something worthwhile when I

_____

_____

I would like to thank the following people for making this accomplishment possible:

_____

_____

_____

Again, thank you so much! It really means a lot to me that _____

_____

RULE #4

During discussions, your child should respect other students' comments, opinions, and ideas. When possible, she should make statements like "I agree with John, and I also feel that . . ." or "I disagree with Sara. She made a good point, but I feel that . . ." or "I think Victor made an excellent observation, and it made me realize . . ."

Activity #1

Does it bother you when someone always tells you that your opinions or ideas are wrong? It bothers other people, too! This exercise will help your child choose the proper thing to say to show respect for the opinions of others, while at the same time expressing her own ideas. Ask her to circle the name of the person who says the sentence that shows that the speaker appreciates what the other person is saying.

SCENE 1: MOVIE MAGIC

Stacy: Did you see that new movie? I thought it was really great!
Taylor: Are you kidding? I thought the movie was horrible!
—OR—

Ron: You're right, Stacy, parts of it were great, but a few things about it
  bothered me.

SCENE 2: SUPER SPORTS

Nelson: I think our team is going to blow the doors off Springfield's team.
Evan: I agree! I think we need to work on defense, but we should beat them.
—OR—
Turner: No way! Our team can't even kick a ball! I think we're going to get
  killed.

SCENE 3: AMAZING AUTHOR

Marisa: I love this author! Don't you think she's just the best?
Carter: I think her stories are boring. I'd much rather read something by
  this guy.
—OR—
Sera: She's not my favorite author, but I agree, she has written some great
  books.

SCENE 4: ELECTION SELECTION

Foster: I can't believe Larry Burton won the class election! I don't think he'll
  be a very good president.
Peter: I was surprised, too. But you never know—he may surprise us.
—OR—
Tanya: Of course he won! His speech was the best, and he's the most pop-
  ular.

SCENE 5: GAME GREATNESS

Kelsey: Have you tried the new video game? I think it's really cool.

David: It's not that cool. I like the original version of the game better.

—OR—

Erin: You're right, it is cool, but there are some things I still like about the original game.

SCENE 6: PIZZA PUZZLE

Christopher: I love Mario's Pizza! My family went there last night for dinner.

Zachary: Blech! Their pizza makes me gag. I'd much rather eat at Ledo's.

—OR—

Caitlin: Mario's is good, but have you ever tried the pizza at Ledo's?

SCENE 7: JOKE JUDGES

Robert: Did you hear Brian's joke? I thought it was hilarious!

Travis: I agree, it was funny. Have you heard this joke? I think it's funny, too.

—OR—

Grace: It wasn't funny at all! It was for babies! This joke is much funnier.

Now write the first letter of each name you circled on the lines below.

This is what you show people when you show them you appreciate what they say:

You show them _____ _____ _____ _____ _____ _____ _____!

Activity #2

Invite your child to practice rephrasing his thoughts and opinions so they sound more respectful of others. Read each dialogue to or with your child. Then have him rewrite the second sentence to make it more respectful. Encourage him to say the new sentence out loud. Remind him that it is okay to share his opinions with others as long as he expresses respect for their opinions, too.

SCENE 1: TEACHER TEST

Carrie: I think Mrs. Appleton is a great teacher.
June: Really? I wish we had Mrs. Tucker.

What would you say? _____

_____

SCENE 2: PITCHING PROBLEMS

Phillip: I can't believe our team traded for such a losing pitcher! We'll never win now!
Melissa: Don't be stupid! That pitcher is great! We're on our way to a championship!

What would you say? _____

_____

SCENE 3: SHOP SHOCKER

Daniel: Have you checked out the new store at the mall? It sells great outdoors stuff.

Ben: I think that store is awful! How can you even shop there?

What would you say? _____

_____

SCENE 4: WEEKEND WHAMMIES

Tracy: My dad's taking me to the park this weekend to go in-line skating. I can't wait!

Randall: How boring! I'd much rather go kayaking than skating.

What would you say? _____

_____

SCENE 5: COOL COUSINS

Sheila: My cousin just arrived from Ireland! She's got all these really great pictures of castles and stuff!

Isaac: Oh yeah? Well, my cousin went to Egypt! He's got pictures of pyramids!

What would you say? _____

_____

RULE #5

If your child wins or does well at something, teach him not to brag. If he loses, teach him not to show anger. Instead, he should say something like "I really enjoyed the competition, and I look forward to playing you again," or "Good game," or he shouldn't say anything at all. To show anger or sarcasm, such as "I wasn't playing hard anyway. You really aren't that good," shows weakness.

Activity #1

Does your child know the appropriate thing to say when winning or losing? Find out! First, read with him all the winning—and losing—situations in the first column. Then read the possible responses in the second column. First, ask him to cross out the responses that would not be appropriate. Then have your child match the appropriate responses for each situation. (Hint! The appropriate responses can really be mixed and matched for the various situations.)

IT'S NOT WHETHER YOU WIN OR LOSE:

Your basketball team wins the state championship. What should you say to your opponent?

Your class wins the math competition. What should you say to the losing class?

Your soccer team loses the first game of the season. What should you say to the winning team?

You win second place in a writing contest. What should you say to the person who wins first place?

Your class elects you as class president. What should you say to the runner-up?

During a timed running of the 40-meter dash, a classmate scores better than you. What should you say to her?

IT'S WHAT YOU SAY AFTERWARD THAT COUNTS!

Good going! You must have studied hard!

Too bad we were better than you!

It was a close election.

It's only the first game. We're just warming up.

Good competition! Those math problems were tough!

I would have won if I had really tried.

Wow! Good race! You're definitely faster than I am!

I would have scored better, but I had a leg cramp.

IT'S NOT WHETHER
YOU WIN OR LOSE:

Your best friend scores better on a spelling test than you do. What do you say to him?

IT'S WHAT YOU SAY
AFTERWARD THAT COUNTS!

Good game. Your new goalie is awesome!

Good job! Your story was really exciting!

I would have scored better if I didn't have a cold.

Good game. We can see why you made it to the state finals.

Activity #2

Invite your child to be gracious when winning *and* losing. Have her complete each award ribbon with something appropriate to say in each situation.

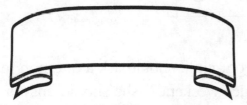

Your softball team beats the team of your rival school. What should you say to the rival team?

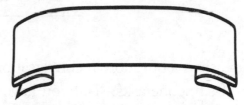

Your poster wins first place in your school's art competition. What should you say to other kids in your class?

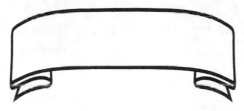

Your group's science project comes in second at the science fair. What should you say to the group that won first place?

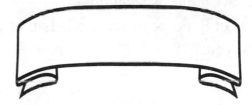

A teammate on the swim team beat the record you set last year for the backstroke. What should you say to him?

RULE #6

When asked a question in conversation, your child should ask a question in return. If someone asks, "Did you have a nice weekend?" she should answer the question and then ask a question in return. For example:

"Did you have a nice weekend?"

"Yes, I had a great time. My family and I went shopping. What about you? Did you have a nice weekend?"

It is only polite to show others that you are just as interested in them as they are in you.

Activity #1

Invite your child to take this quiz to see how well she is able to ask questions of others during a conversation. Have her circle **true** or **false** to show when she asked questions of people in the past. Because this skill takes practice, encourage her to answer honestly, explaining that you don't expect her to ask questions in every situation.

———

Your teacher asks you how your summer vacation was. You tell him you went to the beach, then ask him what he did for his summer vacation.

_____ _____

A relative asks what subject you enjoy most in school. You tell her it's math, then ask her what subject she enjoyed most when she was in school.

_____ _____

A friend asks if you like using your new in-line skates. You tell her all about them, then ask if she has ever tried in-line skating.

_____ _____

Your sister asks how you survived the first day of school. You fill her in on the highs and lows, then ask her how she survived her first day.

_____ _____

Your cousin, who lives in the city, asks what it is like to live in the country. You describe your experiences, then ask him what it's like to live in the city.

_____ _____

Your father comes home from work and asks how your day at school was. After telling a bit about your day, you ask him about his day at work.

_____ _____

A neighbor compliments you on your vegetable garden. You offer some gardening tips, then compliment her on her flower garden and ask for advice.

_____ _____

A friend at school says he likes your sneakers. You
say thank you, then say how much you like his
jacket and ask where he got it.   _____   _____

A friend at another school asks how your class
celebrates a big holiday. After telling a bit about it,
you ask her what her school does.   _____   _____

A friend asks you what you like about collecting
baseball cards. You explain, then ask him why he
thinks collecting stamps is interesting.   _____   _____

NOW SEE HOW YOU SCORE! ADD UP ALL YOUR TRUE STATEMENTS.

If you scored 8–10, you are an expert conversationalist! You always include others in a conversation and never hog up all the talking. Good for you!

If you scored 5–7, you are a quasi-conversationalist. You like to talk about the things you do, but sometimes you forget to ask others about themselves. That's okay! With a little bit of practice, you can become an expert!

If you scored 2–4, you are a talking titan! You like to talk about yourself, but you often forget to include others in the conversation. Try to add a few more questions when you talk to others so they can talk, too.

If you scored 0–1, you are a conversation hog! All you do is talk about yourself. You must make an effort to ask others about things in which they have an interest. Remember to let others talk and be sure to listen carefully to what they have to say.

Activity #2

Present these conversation starters to your child, and ask him to ad-lib a conversation back to you. Encourage him to ask questions to keep the conversation going. Prompt him as necessary. Depending on how well he responds to activities (For example, is he a better oral learner or written learner?), you might let him write his response on the lines provided on this page.

Your teacher: Hi, [insert name]! Did you have fun during the winter break?

You: _____

_____

_____

Your friend: Hey! I didn't see you all weekend. What did you do?

You: _____

_____

_____

Your grandmother, or other relative, on the phone from out of state:
    Hi, [insert name]! What's the weather like by you?

You: _____

_____

_____

Your cousin, or a close friend, that you stay in touch with via e-mail:

Hi, [insert name]! I can't believe school's about to start again. Have you finished all your back-to-school shopping?

You: _____

_____

_____

Your mom or dad: How was the party at [insert name]'s house?

You: _____

_____

_____

RULE #7

Teach your child that, when coughing, sneezing, or burping, it is appropriate to turn his head away from others and cover his mouth with the palm of his hand. Using a fist is not acceptable. Afterward, he should say, "Excuse me."

Activity #1

This is a rule that many families already instill in both parents and kids, but it doesn't hurt to reinforce it! Work with your child to complete each sentence on pages 34–35 with a word from the box. You will use each word only once. When all of the sentences have been completed correctly, two things you can say after coughing, burping, or sneezing appear in the parentheses. Good luck!

bless	burp	cough	cover	expect	good
hand	head	health	hiccups	make	manners
mouth	rude	sick	sneeze	spirits	spit

Puzzle 1:

a. You should cover your mouth when you _____.

b. People_____ you to excuse yourself after you burp.

c. Cover your mouth and say excuse me each time you _____.

d. You should cover your mouth when you _____.

e. Not covering your mouth could make others _____.

f. You can say, "God _____ you!" or "Gesundheit!" after someone sneezes.

g. You don't want to _____ others sick with your germs, do you?

h. Covering your mouth after sneezing is practicing good _____.

____ ____ (____) ____ ____ ____

____ (____) ____ ____ ____ ____

____ ____ (____) ____ ____ ____ ____

____ ____ (____) ____ ____

(____) ____ ____ ____

____ ____ (____) ____ ____

(____) ____ ____ ____

____ (____) ____ ____ ____ ____

Puzzle 2: _____

1. It is _____ manners to cover your mouth when you sneeze or cough.
2. You should also turn your _____ when you sneeze or cough.
3. When you sneeze or cough, you release_____ into the air.
4. You should always excuse yourself after you _____.
5. It shows good_____ when you follow this rule.
6. People will think you are_____ if you don't cover your mouth when you sneeze or cough.
7. You should use the palm of your_____ to cover your mouth when you sneeze or cough.
8. Don't forget to_____ your mouth when you sneeze!
9. You might spread_____ if you do not cover your mouth when you sneeze or cough.
10. You should cover your_____ when you cough, too.

(____) ____ ____ ____

____ (____) ____ ____

(____) ____ ____ ____

____ (____) ____ ____

____ ____ (____) ____ ____ ____ ____

____ ____ (____) ____

(____) ____ ____ ____

____ ____ ____ (____) ____

____ ____ (____) ____ ____ ____ ____

____ ____ ____ (____) ____

Activity #2

Read the following letter from Disgruntled Dora to advice columnist Polly Polite with your child. Talk about the problems raised in the letter. Then work with her to write a letter from Polly to Dora, explaining why people should cover their mouths when sneezing, coughing, or burping. Don't forget to include "Excuse me" and "God bless you!"

Dear Polly,

I am very annoyed! Every time I turn around, people are sneezing or coughing without putting their hands over their mouths or even turning their heads away. And does anyone ever say, "God bless you" anymore? And how about burping! I can't remember the last time I heard someone say "Excuse me!" after burping! Don't people realize that ignoring these little bits of manners is not only rude, but unhealthy? Polly, could you please remind your readers about the importance of following these simple rules of politeness?

Disgruntled Dora

Dear Dora,

_____

_____

_____

_____

_____

RULE #8

Students should never smack their lips, roll their eyes, or show disrespect with gestures.

Activity #1

Smacking lips (also known as the sound "tsk") and rolling eyes might be reactions so ingrained in your child that you don't even notice them anymore. But other people certainly will, which may give them the impression that your child is being disrespectful. Help her eliminate this behavior by reading the short stories below. Ask her to cross out all the instances when the characters make gestures that seem inappropriate or disrespectful. Afterward, review the stories to help your child notice any reactions that she may have missed.

———

Susan couldn't believe it. Her teacher had actually picked someone else for the starring role in the class play.

"Tamika knew all her lines," Mr. Druthers said.

Susan rolled her eyes. "That's easy, Mr. Druthers. But can she act?"

"Tamika will do just fine."

"But I would have done better!" Susan insisted, smacking her lips.

"Perhaps for the next play, you can try harder to remember all the lines."

Susan held up a hand to Mr. Druthers. "Whatever!" Then she stormed off.

———

The score was tied 2–2, and Billy came up to the plate. He swung once, and the ball whizzed past him. He swung twice, and the ball went by him again.

"This time, I'll be patient," Billy said to himself. So he didn't swing.

It didn't matter. The umpire called the pitch a strike, and Billy was out.

"A strike! That wasn't a strike!" Billy hollered as he threw off his batting helmet.

"Yes, son, it was a strike," the umpire said calmly.

"Tsk! It was outside!" Billy mumbled, pointing beyond the side of the plate.

"Son, take your seat," the umpire instructed.

Billy rolled his eyes. "I can't believe this! You must need glasses!"

Billy's coach came out of the dugout.

"Coach, did you see that bad call?" Billy exclaimed, rolling his eyes some more.

"That's enough, Billy," Coach Andrews said. "Now, let's sit down."

Mumbling to himself, Billy walked back to the dugout and kicked the seat.

Cara anxiously waited for the teacher to hand back her composition. She'd worked really hard on it, and she was certain she'd get an A+.

A B– stared her in the face.

Cara marched up to the teacher's desk and threw her paper down on top of it. She smacked her lips and said, "I deserve an A! My composition was great!"

Mrs. Ridley looked thoughtful. Then she said, "Your composition was very good, Cara. I liked the topic. But your grammar needs some work."

Cara rolled her eyes. "Are you kidding? My grammar is perfect!" She folded her arms in front of her chest, stuck out her hip, and began tapping her foot.

"I'm sorry you feel that way, Cara. I marked the places that could use improvement."

Cara rolled her eyes again. "You don't know what you're talking about." She grabbed her paper and marched back to her seat.

Activity #2

What situations cause your child to use inappropriate gestures, to roll his eyes or tsk? Ask him to list circumstances that provoke these reactions from him. Then role-play one of the situations. As your child exhibits the behavior, imitate him right back. This may help him realize how he looks when reacting this way. After the role-play, be sure to try the situation again, this time helping him act out a more appropriate reaction.

MY TOP FIVE LIP-SMACKING, GESTURE-PROVOKING SITUATIONS

1. _____

2. _____

3. _____

4. _____

5. _____

RULE #9

It is appropriate that your child always say "thank you" when the teacher gives him something. There is no excuse for not showing appreciation.

Activity #1

How often does your child say "thank you"? Does he always say "thank you" when you help with homework? Or when he is passed the potatoes at dinner? Or when he receives presents? Invite him to take this quiz to find out! Have him circle the number that best describes each situation, using the scale below:

0—Never
1—Sometimes
2—Often
3—Always

I say "thank you" to the workers in the cafeteria	0	1	2	3
I say "thank you" when I receive a gift.	0	1	2	3
I say "thank you" when someone gives me a ride home from school.	0	1	2	3

I say "thank you" when someone holds the door open for me.	0	1	2	3
I say "thank you" during mealtimes when someone passes me food.	0	1	2	3
I say "thank you" when someone helps me with my homework.	0	1	2	3
I say "thank you" to the cashier at the store.	0	1	2	3
I say "thank you" to the bus driver.	0	1	2	3
I say "thank you" to the librarian for helping me find a book.	0	1	2	3
I say "thank you" to my teachers when they help me with an assignment.	0	1	2	3

HOW THANKFUL ARE YOU? CHECK YOUR SCORE!

25–30: Thanks a lot! You say "thank you" almost all the time. Good for you!

18–24: Thanks! You usually remember to say "thank you," but sometimes you forget. That's okay! Try to throw in a few more "thank-yous" when people do nice things for you.

11–17: Thanks a little! Saying "thank you" is a skill you need to work on. You usually forget, but not always. You might want to role-play saying "thank you" with a friend or someone in your family. This will give you practice for the real thing.

0–10: No, thanks! You definitely need to work on your thanking skills! You rarely say "thank you" at all. People may even think you're mean because you don't say "thank you." Work with your friends, parents, or a teacher to say "thank you" more often.

Activity #2

Who should your child thank nearly every day? With your child, list the people that she comes in contact with who would be glad to hear a "thank you." Don't worry if you don't remember the name of the bus driver or the waiter at the pizza place. Write down who the person is and what he or she does that your child should be thankful for.

I SHOULD SAY
"THANK YOU" TO: BECAUSE . . .

_____   _____

_____   _____

_____   _____

_____   _____

_____   _____

Ask your child to choose one person on the list. Encourage your child to create a thank-you card to give to this person. Make sure your child includes a message that describes the special thing this person does.

RULE #10

When someone gives something to your child, she should never insult that person by making negative comments about the gift or by insinuating that it isn't appreciated.

Activity #1

See if your child can recognize which response is correct and which is inappropriate. Read or role-play the responses of the Toogood Twins below as the twins receive presents. Ask your child to circle or identify the correct response.

1. Timmy and Tammy Toogood both receive striped shirts.

Timmy Says: **Tammy Says:**

"Thanks! I really like stripes!"   "Ick! Stripes are out this year!"

2. Timmy and Tammy Toogood both receive roller skates, not in-line skates.

Timmy says: **Tammy says:**

"No one roller-skates anymore!"   "These look like fun! Thanks!"

3. Timmy and Tammy Toogood both receive stuffed dinosaurs.

Timmy says:
"I'm too old for stuffed animals!"

Tammy says:
"How cute! Thank you!"

4. Timmy and Tammy Toogood both receive a box of crayons.

Timmy says:
"Wow! Look at all the colors! Thanks!"

Tammy says:
"Where's the drawing paper?"

5. Timmy and Tammy Toogood both receive the same book.

Timmy says:
"Gee, I already read this one."

Tammy says:
"Thanks! This book is one of my favorites!"

6. Timmy and Tammy Toogood are both invited to their grandparents' home for the weekend.

Timmy says:
"I can't wait! Thank you!"

Tammy says:
"But I had plans with my friends!"

7. Timmy and Tammy Toogood both receive new bike helmets.

Timmy says:
"Aw, I wanted to pick out my own helmet."

Tammy says:
"Thanks! This is great!"

8. At a friend's house for dinner, Timmy and Tammy Toogood are both served meatloaf.

Timmy says:

"This looks delicious. Thanks!"

Tammy says:

"What's this? I don't like meatloaf."

9. Timmy and Tammy Toogood's parents get them a kitten.

Timmy says:

"A kitten? I wanted a dog!"

Tammy says:

"I love him already! Thank you!"

10. Timmy and Tammy Toogood's grandparents give them each one present for their birthday.

Timmy says:

"Only one? Thanks for nothing!"

Tammy says:

"Thank you so much!"

See how well your child did. Here are the correct answers he should have circled:

1. Timmy
2. Tammy
3. Tammy
4. Timmy
5. Tammy
6. Timmy
7. Tammy
8. Timmy
9. Tammy
10. Tammy

8–10: Good job! You know how to accept gifts and nice things from people!

5–7: Not bad, but you could learn what it's like to be more gracious. Imagine how you would feel if someone didn't like your gift.

0–4: It's likely that you're insulting the giver when you receive a gift. Try being nicer to others when they give you something. If what you are thinking is not nice, then don't say it. Instead, just say "thank you."

Activity #2

Have your child look at the picture in each box and pretend that someone has given that object as a gift or as a kind gesture. In the space provided, have your child write an appropriate response or "thank you." Review her answers to make sure they are not insulting or negative. You can also have her say her response to you.

RULE #11

Encourage your child to surprise others by performing random acts of kindness. Students should go out of their way to do something surprisingly kind and generous for someone at least once a month.

Activity #1

Does your child understand what a random act of kindness is? Help him find out by looking up the definition of each word in the dictionary. Then invite him to write about moments when random acts of kindness touched his own life.

Random: _____

_____

Act: _____

_____

Kindness: _____

_____

In your own words, explain what a "random act of kindness" is:

_____

_____

_____

Think of some occasions when someone performed a random act of kindness for you. Fill in the chart to tell about your experiences.

WHO PERFORMED THE RANDOM ACT OF KINDNESS?	WHAT WAS THE RANDOM ACT OF KINDNESS?	HOW DID THE RANDOM ACT OF KINDNESS MAKE YOU FEEL?

Activity #2

After completing the first activity, review with your child how he felt after each random act of kindness. Help him conclude that random acts of kindness make people feel special. Then discuss people for whom he could perform a random act of kindness. Have him write the name on the first line, then describe the random act of kindness and why the person might like it. The headings below are to get you started.

A Relative: _____

    Random act of kindness: _____

_____

    Why is this act appropriate? _____

_____

A Teacher: _____

    Random act of kindness: _____

_____

    Why is this act appropriate? _____

_____

A School Worker: _____

    Random act of kindness: _____

    _____

    Why is this act appropriate? _____

    _____

A Neighbor: _____

    Random act of kindness: _____

    _____

    Why is this act appropriate? _____

    _____

A Person in the Community: _____

    Random act of kindness: _____

    _____

    Why is this act appropriate? _____

    _____

A Friend: _____

Random act of kindness: _____

_____

Why is this act appropriate? _____

_____

After your child has concluded a random act of kindness, talk with your child about how he feels. Invite him to write his impressions and feelings below.

When I complete a random act of kindness, I feel:

_____

_____

_____

_____

_____

_____

_____

RULE #12

In school, your child may be asked to evaluate another student's work. When grading other students' papers, giving someone an incorrect grade, whether it is higher or lower than the student deserves, is unfair and may result in a penalty to your child's grade. Make your child aware that the only marks she should make on others' papers are an "X" and the number of answers that were incorrect.

Activity #1

Have your child look at the papers on pages 56–59. They have been graded by kids in a classroom. Challenge your child to draw an "X" next to the papers that are marked incorrectly, according to Rule #12. In addition, ask her to circle the marking that is incorrect.

TEST #1

Please solve the below mathematical problems.
Place the answers next to each of the equations. Each answer is worth 10 points.
If the equation is incorrect please write "X" next to the equation; then write
the correct answer.

1. $5 \times 9 =$ *45* √

2. $64 \div 8 =$ *9* X

3. $1345 + 355 =$ *1990* X

4. $114 \div 12 =$ *12* X

5. $6 \times 6 =$ *36* √

6. $45 - 12 =$ *33* √

7. $121 - 28 =$ *93* √

8. $300 + 200 =$ *500* √

9. $2000 + 600 + 48 =$ *264.8* X

10. $1/4 + 1/3 =$ *1/7* X

TEST #1-B

Please solve the below mathematical problems.
Place the answers next to each of the equations. Each answer is worth 10 points.
If the equation is incorrect please write "X" next to the equation; then write
the correct answer.

1. $5 \times 9 =$ *45*

2. $64 \div 8 =$ *9* **X** *answer= 8*

3. $1345 + 355 =$ *1990* **X** *answer= 1700*

4. $114 \div 12 =$ *12* **X** *answer= 144 $\div$ 12= 12*

5. $6 \times 6 =$ *36*

6. $45 - 12 =$ *33*

7. $121 - 28 =$ *93*

8. $300 + 200 =$ *500*

9. $2000 + 600 + 48 =$ *264.8* **X** *answer= 2648*

10. $\frac{1}{4} + \frac{1}{3} =$ *1/7* **X** *answer= 7/12*

TEST #1-C

Please solve the below mathematical problems.

Place the answers next to each of the equations. Each answer is worth 10 points.

If the equation is incorrect please write "X" next to the equation; then write

the correct answer.

WAY TO GO! ☺

1. $5 \times 9 =$ **45** $\checkmark$

2. $64 \div 8 =$ **8** $\checkmark$

3. $1345 + 355 =$ **1700** $\checkmark$

4. $114 \div 12 =$ **NO 144 $\div$ 12 = 12** $\checkmark$

5. $6 \times 6 =$ **36** $\checkmark$

6. $45 - 12 =$ **33** $\checkmark$

7. $121 - 28 =$ **93** $\checkmark$

8. $300 + 200 =$ **500** $\checkmark$

9. $2000 + 600 + 40 + 8 =$ **2648** $\checkmark$

10. $1/4 + 1/3 =$ **7/ 12** $\checkmark$

TEST #1-D

Please solve the below mathematical problems.

Place the answers next to each of the equations. Each answer is worth 10 points.

If the equation is incorrect please write "X" next to the equation; then write the correct answer.

1. $5 \times 9 =$ *48* **X**

2. $64 \div 8 =$ *9* **X**

3. $1345 + 355 =$ *1990* **X**

4. $114 \div 12 =$ *12* **X**

5. $6 \times 6 =$ *66* **X**

6. $45 - 12 =$ *32* **X**

7. $121 - 28 =$ *95* **X**

8. $300 + 200 =$ *600* **X**

9. $2000 + 600 + 40 + 8 =$ *264.8* **X**

10. $^1/_4 + ^1/_3 =$ *1/7* **X**

Try Harder Next Time!

Activity #2

Encourage your child to rewrite Rule #12 in her own words, listing each part of the rule on the lines below. Talk with her about why these rules are important.

Rules for Grading Papers!

#1: Only _____

_____

#2: Never _____

_____

#3: Don't change _____

_____

#4: Don't identify _____

_____

#5: After grading and exchanging papers, treat your classmates _____

_____

Additional advice you would give to kids who grade classmates' papers:

_____

RULE #13

When your child's class reads together, your child must follow along. He must be prepared when called upon and know exactly where to begin immediately reading aloud.

Activity #1

How well does your child pay attention when the teacher reads out loud in class? Invite your child to take this self-help quiz to find out. Have him circle the words that tell what he does during reading. Tell him to be honest!

When the teacher reads in class, I:

. . . listen closely and follow along word for word in my book	Never	Sometimes	Always
. . . think about what is happening in the story and what might happen next.	Never	Sometimes	Always
. . . write down questions to ask about the story or topic.	Never	Sometimes	Always

. . . try to imagine the actions that are taking place.	Never	Sometimes	Always
. . . understand the story or topic so I can contribute to a class discussion.	Never	Sometimes	Always
. . . doodle silly pictures on scrap paper.	Never	Sometimes	Always
. . . stare out the window and daydream.	Never	Sometimes	Always
. . . write notes to my friends.	Never	Sometimes	Always
. . . do my math homework.	Never	Sometimes	Always
. . . pretend I am somewhere else.	Never	Sometimes	Always

HOW DID YOU DO? CHECK YOUR SCORE!

THE FIRST FIVE

▸ If you circled mostly "Sometimes" and "Always" for the first five examples, you actively participate during class readings. Good job!

▸ If you circled mostly "Sometimes" and "Never" for the first five examples, you're not paying much attention during class readings. This is a skill you need to work on.

THE SECOND FIVE

▸ If you circled mostly "Sometimes" and "Always" for the second five examples, your mind is definitely somewhere else during class readings! Try to focus more!

▸ If you circled mostly "Sometimes" and "Never" for the second five examples, your mind is usually on the reading and not somewhere else. Way to go!

Activity #2

Invite your child to read this nonfiction passage to you as you follow along. (You will need to make a copy.) Ask her to observe how well you pay attention. As she reads, exhibit behaviors that show that you are not listening. For example, you might look out the window, doodle, balance your checkbook, or write a grocery list.

Then have your child complete the observation sheet at the bottom of the page, detailing your distracted behavior and what you should do to improve. Afterward, discuss with her the importance of listening during reading time in class.

THE TRUTH ABOUT FOREST FIRES

They can burn steadily for days.

They can threaten homes and businesses.

They can destroy hundreds of acres of wilderness.

Yet for all their destructiveness, some people believe that forest fires are actually necessary for the forest ecosystem. Many people also believe that forest fires can even help the forest by preventing worse fires in the future!

To understand a forest fire, we need to understand the life of a forest. A forest is a living, breathing environment, full of plants and animals. As animals and plants die, they become part of the forest floor. Often, the forest floor becomes so littered with fallen trees and leaves that new plant growth cannot occur. A forest fire can quickly burn away these dead plants, allowing new plants to grow.

The problem with forest fires is that most do not occur naturally. A natural forest fire is one that occurs by a strike of lightning. However, many forest fires are set—either purposely or accidentally—by people.

Whether set by people or set by nature, forest fires can have positive effects on a forest. And, although it may take some time, most forests do recover and grow once again after a fire, no matter how hot the blaze or how fierce the firestorm.

OBSERVATIONS

What did you observe about your parent as you read?
Write your observations below.

Did your parent look at the page while you read? _____

Did your parent jot down any questions or ideas as you read? _____

Do you believe your parent was listening to you read? _____

What behaviors did your parent engage in as you read? List them below.

1. _____

2. _____

3. _____

4. _____

5. _____

What are your recommendations for your parent the next time you read aloud to

him or her? _____

_____

_____

_____

RULE #14

In school, your child should answer all written questions with a complete sentence. For example, if the question is "What is the capital of Russia?" the proper response, in writing, is "The capital of Russia is Moscow." Also, in conversation with others, it is important to use complete sentences out of respect for the other person. If a person asks "How are you?" for example, your child should not just respond with "Fine." Instead, she should say, "I'm doing fine, thank you. How about yourself?"

Activity #1

Help your child practice answering questions in complete sentences by conducting this interview. Suggest that she is being interviewed by a local newspaper or a popular magazine. The reporter is writing a story about local kids and the fun things they do. As you ask each question below, encourage your child to answer with a complete sentence. You can also have her write the answers on the lines.

Reporter: Hello! Thank you for agreeing to talk to me today! My first
question is an easy one. What is your name?

You: _____

Reporter: Great! And where do you live?

You: _____

Reporter: Wonderful! And how old are you?

You: _____

Reporter: Now that we have the basics out of the way, what do you like to do in your community?

You: _____

Reporter: That's very interesting! Which of these activities is the most interesting to you?

You: _____

Reporter: Why is this activity interesting to you?

You: _____

Reporter: Fantastic! Now let's talk about school. Which school do you go to?

You: _____

Reporter: And who is your teacher?

You: _____

Reporter: In which subjects do you think you do the best?

You: _____

Reporter: Thank you very much! This was a great interview!

You: _____

Activity #2

Now invite your child to practice answering the questions below. Tell her that each answer will have four complete sentences, following the four-step technique outlined below. The letters for each question will help her follow each step in order.

THE FOUR STEPS FOR ANSWERING A QUESTION:

    a) Restate the question and give your answer.
    b) Give a reason why you feel that way.
    c) Support your answer.
    d) Restate the question and close.

Question 1: Who do you think is the best professional athlete today?

a) _____

_____

b) _____

_____

c) _____

_____

d) _____

_____

Question 2: Who is your favorite author?

a) _____

_____

b) _____

_____

c) _____

_____

d) _____

_____

Question 3: Which person in your life has the most influence?

a) _____

_____

b) _____

_____

c) _____

_____

d) _____

_____

Question 4: If you could visit any place on Earth, where would you like to go?

a) _____

_____

b) _____

_____

c) _____

_____

d) _____

_____

RULE #15

Throughout the year, your child may receive rewards from you or his teacher for good behavior, academic performances, and other acts worthy of praise. Explain to your child that he should never ask for or demand a reward. It is rude for anyone to ask if they are getting a reward for good behavior. Proper classroom behavior requires students to behave well in school and at home, and do their best because they are trying to better themselves, not because they are anticipating a reward.

Activity #1

How does your child feel he should be rewarded for doing a good job? Find out! Quiz him to determine what he expects for a job well done. Ask him to check off what he expects for each achievement. Then add up the totals and read the score.

You get 100 on a spelling test! As a reward, you expect to get:

_____ five dollars.

_____ out of doing the dishes.

_____ nothing! You should be happy with your accomplishment.

Your soccer team wins a big game! You expect to get:

_____ a pizza party.

_____ a day off from practice.

_____ nothing! You're happy with the win.

You turned in your research report on time! You expect to get:

_____ a dozen cookies.

_____ no more reports for the rest of the year.

_____ nothing! You should always turn in your reports on time.

You've cleaned your room! You expect to get:

_____ a raise in your allowance.

_____ a day at a baseball game.

_____ nothing! Cleaning your room should be an everyday chore.

Your poem is published in a national magazine! You expect to get:

_____ a dinner in your honor.

_____ a story about you in the local newspaper.

_____ nothing! You should feel good about your accomplishment.

Your teacher has selected you to be hall monitor for a week! You expect to get:

_____ special privileges in class.

_____ hot dogs every day in the school cafeteria.

_____ nothing! Being hall monitor is recognition enough.

Your class has sold more candy bars than any other during the school fund drive. You expect to get:

_____ a box of free candy.

_____ a day off from school.

_____ nothing! You were glad to help out.

You got an A on your essay. You expect to get:

_____ published in the school newspaper.

_____ a new set of pens.

_____ nothing! The good grade is reward enough.

You saved a family of baby rabbits from your pet cat. You expect to get:

_____ a parade in your honor.

_____ the key to the city.

_____ nothing! You feel good knowing you saved the rabbits.

Your class scored well on an important statewide test. You expect to get:

_____ an entire day of recess.

_____ a visit from the town mayor.

_____ nothing! Praise and kind words are all you need.

CHECK YOUR SCORE:

▸ If you mostly checked the last answer for each question, good job! You know that the best reward is doing well, and you don't expect to be rewarded every time you achieve something special.

▸ If you checked a combination of the first, second, and third lines for each question, you often expect a reward. Try to see the feeling of accomplishment as the reward and anything else you receive as an extra pat on the back.

▸ If you didn't check any last answers for the questions, you always expect to receive a reward when you do something good. Although it's nice to get something special in return for doing something special, achieving a special goal should be reward enough.

_____

Activity #2

Talk with your child about her special accomplishments, and have her write about them below. Then ask her to list the reward she received for the accomplishment, if any, as well as how she feels about the achievement. Help her understand that the feeling of accomplishment is often reward enough for a job well done. Your child does not need to fill in the entire page; rather, return to the page the next time she reaches a goal.

My Special Accomplishment: _____

Reward: _____

How I felt when I achieved this accomplishment: _____

_____

Why did I feel this way? _____

_____

My Special Accomplishment: _____

Reward: _____

How I felt when I achieved this accomplishment: _____

_____

Why did I feel this way? _____

_____

My Special Accomplishment: _____

Reward: _____

How I felt when I achieved this accomplishment: _____

_____

Why did I feel this way? _____

_____

RULE #16

Your child should understand that homework is to be turned in each day for each subject without exception.

Activity #1

Following your child's homework assignments is one way to monitor her progress and stay aware of her behavior in school.

Pages 76–77 have been set up as a homework log. Sit down each day with your child and fill out the log with the assignments she must complete that night. She need not complete the assignments right away, but now you know what she needs to do during homework time. Make copies of this blank log to use every day, and keep them in a homework folder. Your child may want to fill it out at school.

MY HOMEWORK LOG

What homework do I have for math? _____

_____

What homework do I have for language arts? _____

_____

What homework do I have for spelling? _____

_____

What homework do I have for reading? _____

_____

What homework do I have for social studies/geography? _____

_____

What homework do I have for science? _____

_____

Any other schoolwork:

_____

_____

_____

Activity #2

Keep a running record of how many days in a row your child can consistently complete his homework and turn it in on time. Challenge him to keep the streak alive by recording the dates and assignments below. You might also record his grades on homework assignments, if grades were given. Good luck!

HOMEWORK TRACKER

DATE	HOMEWORK	TURNED IN ON TIME	GRADE

RULE #17

In school, when your child's class changes from one subject to another, the transition should be swift, quiet, and orderly. He should be consistently able to turn from one book to another, complete with all homework and necessary materials, as quickly as possible. The opportune amount of time to spend in transition should be less than ten seconds, working toward a goal of seven seconds.

Activity #1

The few minutes it takes to switch from one subject to another in class are minutes of lost learning time. Remind your child of class time-wasters by asking him to complete the puzzle below. The answer revealed on the next page tells how long it should take him to put away his materials for one subject and get out his materials for the next.

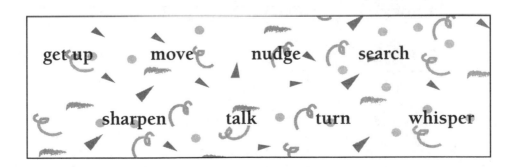

get up   move   nudge   search

sharpen   talk   turn   whisper

When you _____ to your friends between subjects, you waste time.

Even a _____ is a time-waster.

You shouldn't poke or _____ your friends to get their attention.

_____ your pencils before class to save time.

Do not _____ between subjects.

You should only _____ to get out the materials you need for the next subject.

If you need to _____ for your materials, you are wasting time.

If you _____ around to talk to your friends, you're wasting class time, too.

How many seconds should it take to put away materials for one subject and get out the materials for the next?

It should only take _____ or, even better, _____ seconds!

Activity #2

Helping out in the classroom is a way to save time. Exchange ideas with your child about ways that she could help her teacher at school, such as setting up a projector or restocking classroom materials. Have your child list ideas and explain why each would be helpful and how each might save time.

HOW I COULD HELP OUT IN CLASS

1. I could _____ .

   This would be helpful because _____

   _____ .

   _____ .

2. I could _____ .

   This would be helpful because _____

   _____ .

3. I could _____ .

   This would be helpful because _____

   _____ .

4. I could _____ .

   This would be helpful because _____

   _____ .

5. I could _____ .

   This would be helpful because _____

   _____ .

RULE #18

Your child must make very effort to be as organized as possible.

Activity #1

How organized is your child? Does she think she is organized? Invite her to find out with this quiz. Ask her to check **true** or **false** about herself in each situation below. Then review the score with her to see how organized she is.

	TRUE	OR	FALSE?
You always know where your homework assignments are.		_____	_____
You can always find a pen or a sharpened pencil to write with.		_____	_____
You can easily find the book your teacher asks for.		_____	_____
You know when each homework assignment is due.		_____	_____

If you need a ruler for a project, you can easily
find one.   _____   _____

You know which folders hold which papers.   _____   _____

You rarely run out of school supplies.   _____   _____

You are able to quickly find an assignment from last
week.   _____   _____

No matter how clean or messy, you know where
everything in your desk or binder is.   _____   _____

If a new student arrived in class, you could quickly
and easily tell him what he needs for school.   _____   _____

CHECK YOUR SCORE:

8–10 Trues: If you checked 8–10 trues, you're an organizational whiz! You're extremely organized, and it takes you no time at all to get the materials you need. Way to go!

5–7 Trues: If you checked 5–7 trues, you're an organizational whiz-in-training! You're organized with some things, but not with others. Try to work on the items you checked "false," and you'll soon be at whiz status.

0–4 Trues. If you checked 0–4 trues, you're an organizational newbie! It might help you to observe people who are more organized than you to learn how you can be more organized. But don't worry! Being organized is a skill, and one that you can master.

Activity #2

To help your child become more organized, have him complete this checklist every night or morning before school. Discuss where homework assignments, writing paper, pens, pencils, and other supplies should be stored so he can take them to school. Then review the checklist, and help him make sure everything is in its place and ready for school time.

ORGANIZATION CHECKLIST

_____ I have all my homework assignments.

_____ My homework assignments are in my _____ .

_____ All my pencils are sharpened.

_____ I have clean writing paper.

_____ Additional supplies I need for school: _____

_____

_____ .

_____ I also have a pack of tissues.

_____ Do I need any notes or permission slips signed for school?

_____ My notes or permissions slips are in my _____ .

_____ All my school supplies are in my _____ .

_____ I am ready to go to school!

RULE #19

Your child should understand that when homework is assigned, there is to be no moaning or complaining.

Activity #1

Wouldn't it be great if we could all sit around and do nothing all day long? If our time was our own and we didn't feel obligated to teachers, bosses, relatives, even friends? The truth, though, is that we all must do things we don't enjoy, including homework. Your child probably doesn't realize how negative he sounds when he complains about homework or doing chores around the house.

Invite him to find out! Role-play the scenarios below, with your child taking the adult role and you playing the child's role. Each time you are asked to do something, whine and moan and complain. Then discuss how your child feels about your reactions. Encourage him to write down his feelings on the lines below.

#1 Teacher: All right, everyone! I want you to write a 200-word essay about who your favorite relative is and why.

#2 Parent: I would really appreciate it if you would help out with the garage sale today.

#3 Sibling: I'm really stuck with this homework assignment. Can you help?

#4 Grandparent: Do you think you would have time to help me weed my garden?

#5 Boss: Martin called in sick, so I'll need you to keep an eye not only on the register, but on the customers, too.

How did it feel when the person you spoke to moaned, whined, and complained?

_____

_____

Activity #2

Invite your child to think back on any tasks she was asked to perform this week. Discuss the following questions and subsequent answers with your child.

#1 Think about the last time you whined or complained when your parent or teacher asked you to do something. What were the consequences of your complaining?

#2 What might have happened differently if you had agreed to your task without complaining or whining about it?

#3 Do you think the person asking you to do something would have noticed if your reaction had been more positive and accommodating?

#4 What might the consequences of a positive response from you bring?

#5 Which set of consequences do you prefer and why?

RULE #20

Your child should follow the same rules with a substitute teacher as she does with the regular teacher. (This rule is hard for kids, but it is important.)

Activity #1

Kids might think it's fun to goof off when a substitute teacher takes their class, but if you ask them to analyze what's really going on, they might come to a different conclusion. Invite your child to complete the multiple-choice quiz below. Tell her to answer honestly! Then talk about the results.

1. When your class has a substitute teacher, you begin a spitball battle. The teacher:
   a) is happy and joins in
   b) is stressed out and upset
   c) doesn't care

2. You ignore the assignments and lessons given by the substitute. What happens instead?
   a) You catch up with your friends on gossip.
   b) You empty your notebook and reorganize your desk.
   c) You miss an opportunity to learn something new.

3. Because you have a substitute teacher, your class is loud and rowdy. The principal walks by and witnesses your behavior. You feel:

a) proud

b) excited

c) embarrassed

4. Your teacher finds out that you misbehaved with the substitute. Your teacher probably feels:

a) disappointed in you

b) glad he or she missed the bad behavior

c) proud of you

5. Your teacher finds out that you misbehaved with the substitute. You:

a) feel overjoyed

b) feel ashamed

c) don't care

6. You receive extra homework or detention for acting up with the substitute. You feel:

a) awful for misbehaving and getting caught

b) great—you love extra work

c) good—you'll be with your friends at detention

Review your answers. What conclusions can you draw about misbehaving with a

substitute? _____

_____

_____

_____

Activity #2

Encourage your child to imagine that he is a substitute teacher. Have him write two letters to the regular teacher, describing the bad and the good behavior of the class while the regular teacher was away. Then ask your child which letter he, as a student, would like the regular teacher to receive, and discuss why.

Letter #1: Describe a class that misbehaves for the substitute teacher.

Dear _____, [regular teacher's name]

I was very _____ today. The children in your class _____

_____

_____

_____

_____

_____

I hope the next time I have a much _____ experience with your class.

Yours truly,

_____ [name of substitute teacher]

Letter #2: Describe a class that behaves well for the substitute teacher.

Dear _____, [regular teacher's name]

I was very _____ today. The children in your class _____

_____

_____

_____

_____

_____

I wish all my experiences could be as _____ as this one!

Yours truly,

_____ [name of substitute teacher]

RULE #21

Your child must follow classroom protocol. He needs to be organized, efficient, and on task in the classroom. He needs to be aware of proper classroom behavior:

a. Do not get out of your seat without permission. Exception: If you are sick, leave immediately.
b. Do not speak unless:
1. You raise your hand and are called upon by your teacher.
2. Your teacher asks you a question and you are responding.
3. It is recess or lunch.
4. The teacher instructs you otherwise (for example, during group work).

Activity #1

The need to speak, get up, and move about whenever we feel like it can sometimes be overpowering. Yet remaining seated—or silent—shows great patience and respect for rules and others. See if your child knows when he should—and should not—speak or stand up in class. Have him read the list of classroom circumstances below, then circle the letters for the times when he is permitted to speak or stand up. Then have him unscramble the circled letters and write them on the lines at the bottom of the page. If all the answers have been circled correctly, the letters will reveal something your child has.

The following rules must be followed for standing up and speaking in class:

a. You are not allowed to get out of your seat without permission.

b. You can speak if you raise your hand and the teacher calls on you.

c. You can speak at any time to the student next to you.

d. You can stand up when you feel the need to stretch.

e. You can speak during recess.

f. You are allowed to use the pencil sharpener at any time.

g. You are allowed to speak when another student is talking.

h. You can speak during group work.

i. If you feel sick, stand up and leave immediately.

j. If you feel thirsty, stand up and go to the water fountain.

k. You may speak if you see something interesting outside the classroom window.

l. You may stand up if your foot falls asleep.

m. The only time you can leave the room is if you need to go to the bathroom.

n. It is okay to whisper during reading time.

o. It is okay to talk during lunch.

p. It is okay to stand or talk during a classmate's presentation.

q. You are allowed to stand when you want to get the teacher's attention.

r. You are allowed to speak if the teacher asks you a question and you are responding.

s. You are allowed to move around the room when you feel fidgety.

t. You can go to the bookshelf at any time to find something to read.

u. You may speak if a student asks you a question.

v. You are allowed to speak when the teacher instructs you to do so.

Now unscramble the circled letters to complete this sentence:

If you follow these rules, you have good classroom

_____ _____ _____ _____ _____ _____ _____ _____ .

Activity #2

Suggest to your child that she is the president of a club and ask your child to write and deliver a speech, welcoming members to the club. As you listen to the speech, interrupt her, breaking the rules for Rule #21. For example, you might stand up and walk around, talk to someone beside you, ask a question without raising your hand, and so on. Talk with your child about why this behavior is disruptive and how it makes her feel. Then ask her to demonstrate the proper protocol for meetings and classes.

WELCOME TO THE CLUB!

I am your club president, _____. The purpose of this club is to

_____ .

As club members, we will _____

_____ .

During club meetings, I expect all members to _____

_____

_____ .

The reason for such behavior is _____

_____

_____

_____ .

Thanks for joining the club! I'm sure we will have a great year!

RULE #22

Different teachers have different policies regarding food and drink in the classroom. Encourage your child to find out what her teacher's preferences are. Once your child knows the food and drink policy, she can follow the rules associated with it.

Activity #1

Having your favorite foods with you is like having a piece of home by your side. It's comforting. If your child could keep ten favorite foods at her desk at school, which foods would they be? Let her list her favorite comfort foods below.

THESE ARE A FEW OF MY FAVORITE FOODS!

1. _____

2. _____

3. _____

4. _____

5. _____

Activity #2

Have your child write a brief description of his teacher's policy on food and drink in the classroom. Then have him suggest foods he would and wouldn't be allowed to bring to school according to the policy. Ask him to set up a schedule of snack foods he can bring in each day for a week. Work with him to assess whether or not he is following the rules.

SCHOOL FOOD POLICY :_____

_____

SNACK FOOD SCHEDULE :_____

_____

MONDAY :_____

TUESDAY :_____

WEDNESDAY :_____

THURSDAY :_____

FRIDAY :_____

RULE #23

Students should quickly learn the names of other teachers in the school and greet them by saying things like "Good morning, Mrs. Graham" or "Good afternoon, Ms. Ortiz. That is a very pretty dress." (Note: If your child is in line with the rest of the class, the no-talking rule is in effect. However, he should be encouraged to speak to other teachers when entering or leaving school, at recess, on an errand, or changing classes.)

Activity #1

Invite your child to fill in the greetings below to an adult that he knows in school or in the community. Encourage him to include a complimentary sentence, too.

"Good morning, _____ . That's a very nice _____

_____ ."

"Good morning, _____ . I really enjoyed your _____

_____ ."

"Hello, _____ . You look very _____

_____ ."

"Hello, _____ . [Now try a sentence of your own!]

_____ ."

"Hello, _____ . [Write a sentence of your own!]

_____ ."

Activity #2

The greetings in the previous activity are mature and respectful, and adults love to hear them. Help your child practice including these greetings in her everyday speech by role-playing. Then, when you think she should be able to say these greetings on her own, without prompting, chart her progress. Share the chart below with her. Then work with her to fill in the chart each time you notice her saying—or not saying!—a mature greeting.

NAME OF ADULT	DID YOU SAY A FORMAL GREETING? YES/NO	WHAT WAS YOUR GREETING?	WHAT WAS YOUR COMPLIMENT?

RULE #24

Your child should know to always flush a toilet and wash her hands after using the restroom. Explain to her that, in a public restroom, she should get a paper towel before washing. After her hands are clean, she should use the paper towel to turn off the faucets and to press the dispenser to get another paper towel to dry her hands. It is not sanitary to touch areas with clean hands that others have touched with dirty hands.

Activity #1

Public restrooms can be scary places, thriving with germs and bacteria. How often does your child practice germ-fighting techniques? Find out! Ask her to circle **Always, Sometimes**, or **Never** to tell how often she practices the safeguarding rules below.

1. I flush the toilet when I am through using it.	Always	Sometimes	Never
2. I use a paper towel to touch the toilet handle.	Always	Sometimes	Never
3. I wash my hands after using the toilet.	Always	Sometimes	Never

4. I use soap when I wash my hands.	Always	Sometimes	Never
5. I use a paper towel to turn off the faucet after washing my hands.	Always	Sometimes	Never
6. I use a paper towel to press the lever to get a clean paper towel.	Always	Sometimes	Never
7. I dry my hands after washing them, using a clean paper towel.	Always	Sometimes	Never
8. I throw away the paper towel in the trash can.	Always	Sometimes	Never
9. I leave the restroom as neat and as germ-free as I can.	Always	Sometimes	Never

CHECK YOUR SCORE!

If you scored mostly *Always*: You rule the restroom! You know how to protect yourself from unhealthy germs and bacteria, as well as how to protect others by leaving the restroom clean after you use it. You rule!

If you scored mostly *Sometimes*: Not bad! You could improve your restroom visits by being a bit more aware of germs and bacteria, but for the most part, you follow the proper procedures. The next time you use a public restroom, try to remember that germs can make you sick—and germs love public restrooms! So grab those paper towels and protect yourself!

If you scored mostly *Never*: Beware! Your habits are inviting germs and bacteria to attach themselves to you. The best way to prevent germs and bacteria from making themselves at home is to fight them off by flushing them down the toilet and washing them off your hands. Paper towels are a good defense, too! To stay healthy, try to practice more germ-fighting techniques the next time you use a public restroom.

Activity #2

Read the restroom scenarios with your child below. Help him choose the correct answer and circle the letter. If he answers all the questions correctly, a secret message will be revealed at the bottom of the page.

1. If you think touching the handle of the toilet is gross, you can:
   t. flush using a paper towel.
   u. not flush at all.
   v. flush with your pinky.

2. The reason you need to flush is that:
   d. flushing looks neater.
   e. you flush away germs.
   f. flushing wastes water.

3. When you finish, you should:
   p. leave immediately.
   q. wash your hands.
   r. grab a paper towel.

4. You should always wash your hands with water and:
   l. paper towels.
   m. soap.
   n. lotion.

5. You then use the paper towel you got before washing your hands to:
   i. turn off the faucet.
   j. wash your face.
   k. clean the sink.

6. You can use the same paper towel to:

    l. get another paper towel.

    m. turn on the air dryer.

    n. both l and m.

7. After using the paper towels, you should:

    a. throw them away.

    b. save them for next time.

    c. leave them on the floor.

8. If you are afraid to touch the doorknob of the restroom, you could:

    s. open it with your foot.

    t. use a paper towel.

    u. use the hem of your shirt.

9. Following these restroom procedures helps you fight:

    m. crime.

    n. bad grades.

    o. germs and bacteria.

10. Following these restroom procedures makes the restroom:

    q. a dirtier place.

    r. a healthier place.

    s. a scarier place.

Now write the letters you circled in the spaces below, in order, to find out what you are:

You are a germ

____ ____ ____ ____ ____ ____ ____ ____ ____ ____!

RULE #25

Your child's classroom will often have visitors. Your child should understand the protocol regarding visitors: Your child should be prepared to shake hands, introduce himself to the visitor, and welcome the person to school.

Activity #1

Encourage your child to create a welcome sign for a school visitor. Have your child illustrate the sign below, filling in the school name and anything special he would like to tell about the school.

WELCOME
TO

Our school is special because:

▶ _____

▶ _____

▶ _____

Activity #2

Encourage your child to think about what it must be like to be new to school or visiting a school. Have her list the things that would be worrisome or confusing on that first day.

If I were new to our school or visiting, these things would worry or confuse me:

1. _____

2. _____

3. _____

4. _____

5. _____

Now invite your child to role-play being a member of the school welcoming committee as you act as a new kid in school or a school visitor. Have your child guide you through the school, pointing out the things about the school that she is proud of, as well as the things that could be confusing. Let her write down ideas to share on the lines below, in the order of how the new student or school visitor would experience them.

Good morning _____ ! Welcome to _____ !

The first thing you will notice is that _____ .

Don't worry! It's not that confusing. If we go down this hallway, you'll find the

_____ .

Over here, we have the _____ . This is where you will

_____ .

Also, our school has _____

_____

_____

_____

_____

_____

_____

RULE #26

Your child should not save seats in the lunchroom. If other students want to sit down, she should let them and not try to exclude anyone. Students in a school function as a family, and they must treat each other with respect and kindness.

Activity #1

It's tough to break away from one's clique. Even as adults, we have friends or groups that are more special to us than others. In school, these cliques can be very important to kids. But just as cliques include some people, more often than not they exclude others. And feeling excluded—whether in the classroom, at the lunch table, or during recess—is extremely detrimental to self-esteem. Is your child a friend to all or a friend to only a select few? Encourage her to find out by completing this quiz.

1. For a class project, you're assigned a partner. You're not really friends with this person, so you:
   a) ignore him and work on the project by yourself. (1)
   b) only speak to him when absolutely necessary. (2)
   c) talk openly with him to get ideas for the project. (3)

2. A new kid in class has joined your reading group. You:
   a) encourage her to be part of the discussion. (3)
   b) pretend she isn't there. (1)
   c) let her speak when she has the guts to jump in. (2)

3. A kid in class tries to join your table at lunch. You:
   a) tell him that all the seats are taken. (1)
   b) move over to make room. (3)
   c) only let him sit if he has some good food to share. (2)

4. You notice a kid watching you and your friends play basketball at recess. You:
   a) invite her to join the game. (3)
   b) invite her to keep score. (2)
   c) show off so she thinks that you're the best. (1)

5. At recess, a kid asks if he can join your friends playing kickball. You:
   a) laugh with your friends and continue to play. (1)
   b) explain that teams have already been picked, but maybe tomorrow. (2)
   c) gladly let him play. (3)

6. In the lunchroom, you notice that a new kid isn't sure where to sit. You:
   a) pretend you didn't notice; after all, it's not your problem. (1)
   b) wave and ask if she would like to join you and your friends. (3)
   c) ask your friends if they want to invite her to sit at the table. (2)

7. Your teacher assigns seats in class, and someone you don't know is seated next to you. You:
   a) smile and introduce yourself. (3)
   b) grin and bear it. (2)
   c) frown and scowl. (1)

8. Your teacher tells the class to count off to form groups. All the number 1s will be one group, the number 2s another group, and so on. You:

   a) get in line quietly and count when it is your turn. (3)

   b) try to organize your friends so you'll all have the same number. (1)

   c) moan and complain about how unfair this system is, but do it anyway. (2)

9. Your best friend is late for lunch, and someone wants to sit in his seat. You:

   a) politely explain that the seat has been saved. (2)

   b) roll your eyes and explain that your best friend sits there. (1)

   c) let the new person sit there, then make room when your friend arrives. (3)

10. You and your friends are hanging out at recess, when you notice a new kid reading by herself. You:

    a) shrug and assume that she really likes to read. (2)

    b) point and tell your friends that she looks like a snob. (1)

    c) Say, "Excuse me," and ask the reader if she would like to join you; after all, maybe she is just shy. (3)

CHECK YOUR SCORE!

26–30: Awesome! You don't like to exclude people, even if you don't know them. Sometimes you may even go out of your way to be friendly and include other people. You're really nice to everyone.

21–25: Good! Usually you think to include others, and you usually don't mind if someone new joins your group. You might tend to be shy yourself, so sometimes you have a hard time being the one to take the initiative to make others feel welcome. Try not to be! Everyone likes to feel that they are part of the family.

15–20: So-So! You feel comfortable with your group of friends, and sometimes you may feel uncomfortable when someone new tries to join in. Making yourself—and others—feel comfortable with new friends is something you need to work on. It shouldn't be that hard, though! Instead of feeling uncomfortable when your teacher assigns you to a group of people you don't know, look at it as an adventure. What can you learn from them?

10–14: Oh, no! You're not a very welcoming person. You like your friends, and you don't think anyone should intrude on those friendships. You need to learn to accept others into your group. You'll meet people your entire life. Some you will like and some you won't. Some may not like you. Learning how to accept and learn from people other than your friends will make you a better-rounded individual.

Activity #2

Tell your child that this rectangle below represents a lunch table. Invite him to write in the names of the kids that he sits with at lunch.

_____ _____ _____ _____

```
+------------------------------------------------+
|                                                |
|                                                |
|                                                |
|                 MY LUNCH TABLE                 |
|                                                |
|                                                |
|                                                |
+------------------------------------------------+
```

_____ _____ _____ _____

Now have your child create a seating chart for a new group of friends at the lunch table on the next page. Tell him to choose two or three friends from the original lunch table, then to include two or three new friends that usually don't sit there. Compare the two lunch tables with him, and ask him what could be fun about sitting with new kids at lunch.

NEW LUNCH TABLE #1

Try it again! Write in some new friends on this table, too.

NEW LUNCH TABLE #2

RULE #27

Your child should not look at another student who is being disciplined. Your child wouldn't want others looking at him if he were in trouble or being reprimanded, so he shouldn't look at others in that situation. If he is the student being disciplined, he should not get angry or fuss at students who are looking at him. He should let the teacher handle the situation.

Activity #1

Gently ask your child if he has ever been in trouble at school. How did he feel? What did the other kids do? If your child has not been in trouble, ask him to imagine how it feels to be scolded in class while the rest of the class watches. Then ask him to write a journal entry about the experience on the lines on the next page. Encourage him to write about what he did, how the kids in class reacted, and how he felt while being scolded. Make sure he understands that no one—not even adults—enjoys being corrected or reprimanded while others watch. If your child can't relate to being scolded in class, ask him to do this activity from the perspective of someone in class who does get scolded.

Date: _____

Dear Diary,

Today was just _____ !
        (descriptive word)

I did _____.
        (What did you do?)

My teacher, _____, yelled at me in front of the whole class.
        (teacher's name)

Everyone in class _____ .

I felt so _____ .
        (emotion words)

(Explain what you did and how you felt!) _____

_____

_____

_____

_____

_____

Here's a picture of me when I was being scolded:

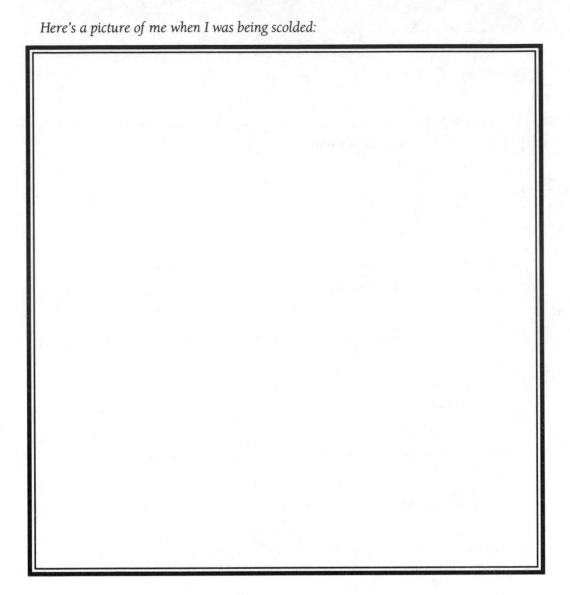

Activity #2

Invite your child to crack this secret code. The letters in the squares tell students what they should do when someone in class gets yelled at. Starting with square one, instruct your child to count five squares, circle the letter, and then write it down.

Tell her to count five more squares, circle the letter, and write it down. Keep going! When all the squares have been circled, the secret message will be revealed! The first few letters have been done for you.

```
1       2       3       4       5
E       T       T       S      (D)      N       R       A              G
E                                                                     (O)
R                                                                      O
S                                                                      O
N                                                                      R
H                                                                      E
L                                                                      N
E                                                                      T
T       I       W       B       H       O       T       E              U
```

D O ___ ___ ___   ___ ___ ___ ___

___ ___ ___ ___   ___ ___ ___ ___ ___

___ ___ ___   ___ ___

___ ___ ___ ___ ___ ___ ___!

RULE #28

If your child has a question about her homework, encourage her to call the teacher. If the teacher is not there to answer the phone, your child should leave a message in the following manner: "Hi, Mr. Clark, this is _____ . I need help with the _____ homework. You can call me back until _____:00. Thank you." There is no need to leave this message more than once.

Activity #1

Not all teachers choose to give their home phone numbers to their students. However, if you teacher does, your child needs to know the proper phone etiquette for placing a call and leaving a message. Have her fill in the message below with the correct information. Then role-play using the phone and leaving a message, encouraging her to read the message she has completed below.

"Hi, _____ (name of your teacher). This is _____

(your name). I need help with the _____

(describe the project) homework assignment. You can call me back at _____ (your number) until ___:00 (time). It is _____ now (current time). Thank you."

Let your child try this exercise again. Have your child choose another teacher from school and another homework assignment to complete the message.

"Hi, _____ (name of your teacher). This is _____

(your name). I need help with the _____

(describe the project) homework assignment. You can call me back at _____

(your number) until ___:00 (time). It is _____ now (current time). Thank you."

You might wish to complete the following chart with the phone numbers of teachers who allow your child to call with questions.

TEACHER	SUBJECT	PHONE NUMBER
_____	_____	_____
_____	_____	_____
_____	_____	_____
_____	_____	_____
_____	_____	_____

Activity #2

Just because a teacher offers his or her home phone number does not mean your child has permission to call whenever he feels like it! Have him check the appropriate column to show that he knows when it is appropriate to call the teacher.

	APPROPRIATE	INAPPROPRIATE
1. You don't understand how you should choose your topic for an English composition.	_____	_____
2. You forgot to write down the words for your spelling test.	_____	_____
3. You need to share the latest gossip.	_____	_____
4. You need help getting started with a social studies project.	_____	_____
5. You need to choose which clothes to wear to a school party.	_____	_____
6. You need extra help solving a difficult math problem.	_____	_____
7. You have trouble coming up with an idea for the school science fair.	_____	_____

8. You forgot which pages you should
read over the weekend.   _____   _____

9. You and your best friend have a fight,
and you need advice.   _____   _____

10. You're not sure how to use latitude
and longitude on a map.   _____   _____

Review your child's answers. Talk about why it is inappropriate to call the teacher in some situations. Then have your child identify a person that he could call for answers or help with these situations.

1. _____

2. _____

3. _____

4. _____

5. _____

RULE #29

Your child should learn acceptable manners during mealtimes. The following are the ABCs of Food Etiquette.

Activity #1

The ABCs of Food Etiquette are written below. Have your child complete each rule with the correct word. Then challenge him to find and circle the words in the word-find puzzle on page 126. (Hint! If you are not sure of an answer, try to find an appropriate word in the word find.)

A. When you first sit down for a meal, immediately place your _____ in your lap. If your silverware is wrapped in a napkin, unwrap it as soon as you sit down and place the napkin in your lap.

B. When you are finished eating, place your napkin on the table to the left of your plate. Don't crumple it, because you don't want to seem untidy. Never leave your napkin on your _____ . This implies that the napkin is too dirty to be left on the table.

C. Never place your elbows on the _____ .

D. Use one _____ to eat, unless you are cutting or buttering food. Never have your fork in one hand and a glass in the other.

E. Do not lick your _____ . There is a napkin provided for the purpose of cleaning your fingers. There is no need to lick yourself clean.

F. Do not smack your _____ and chew noisily.

G. Do not chew with your mouth _____ .

H. Do not _____ with your mouth full. Sometimes people will place a hand over their mouth and talk anyway. Don't do that. Wait until you have swallowed your food to speak.

I. If something is caught in your _____ , wait until you are in the restroom to remove it.

J. Do not _____ [when you drink or eat soup].

K. Do not _____ with your food.

L. If you drop your fork, napkin, or anything else on the _____ , do not pick it up. It is very rude and unsanitary to place something on the table that has been on the floor. If you pick up something that has dropped and hand it to a waiter, then you will need to excuse yourself and wash your hands before continuing with your meal. The best way to handle the situation is to leave the item on the floor and ask a waiter for a replacement.

M. You can use your _____ for eating almost everything. There are ten types of foods for which you may use your hands to eat.

N. Never reach over someone's plate to get something. You should say, "Will you _____ pass the salt?"

O. Never start eating from your tray until you are at your _____ .

P When you are eating at a restaurant, you are not to begin eating until all the people at the table have _____ their food.

Q. You should never _____ if the line is too long, if the food isn't good, or if there is a wait. You don't want to be so negative that you spoil the enjoyment of the event for others.

R. If you are unsure which _____ to use, start with the fork, knife, or spoon that is the farthest from your plate. On the left, your salad fork is on the outside and your dinner fork on the inside. On the far right is your soupspoon. Beside it is the spoon you will use to stir coffee or tea, then your salad knife, and then your dinner knife. The utensils above your plate are to be used for dessert.

S. When you are finished eating, do not push your _____ away from you. Leave it where it is in the setting. If you want to show you have finished eating, lay your fork and knife together diagonally across the plate. Place the fork with the tines down and the sharp side of the knife facing you. Of the two utensils, the fork should be closest to you.

T. Never place a piece of silverware that you have _____ back on the table. Leave it on a plate or saucer.

U. If you didn't use a utensil, do not place it on a plate or saucer when you are finished. Just _____ it where it is.

V. Always look a _____ in the eyes when you are ordering, asking a question, or saying "thank you."

W. Make a point to remember the server's _____ if he or she gives it. Use the name as often as possible throughout the course of the meal.

X. If you have to go to the restroom, you should stand up and say "_____ me" as you leave the table.

Y. When you are offered desserts or asked "What sides would you like?" or "What dressing would you like for your salad?" it is best to respond, "What are my _____?" That way, you won't go through a process of naming things the restaurant might not have.

Z. Never talk to the people who serve your food as if they are servants. Treat them with _____ and kindness, and remember, they are the ones who are arranging your food and bringing it to you. You do not want to be on the bad side of a server.

Now circle the words in the puzzle on the next page.

Write the letters you **did not** circle, in order, on the lines below to reveal five foods you can eat with your fingers.

You can eat these foods with your fingers:

____ ____ ____ ____ ____ , ____ ____ ____ ____ ____ ,

____ ____ ____ ____ ____ ____ ____ ,

____ ____ ____ ____ ____ , and

____ ____ ____   ____ ____ ____ ____ .

S	I	L	V	E	R	W	A	R	E	U	P
L	I	H	A	N	D	Z	T	E	E	T	H
U	Z	C	O	M	P	L	A	I	N	E	A
R	F	H	B	A	L	I	B	C	A	N	O
P	L	A	Y	N	E	P	L	C	P	S	O
L	O	I	O	O	A	S	E	K	K	I	P
A	O	R	I	R	S	E	A	T	I	L	T
T	R	E	S	E	E	O	P	E	N	S	I
E	X	C	U	S	E	F	T	A	L	K	O
U	S	E	D	P	L	E	A	V	E	N	S
F	I	N	G	E	R	S	R	I	E	A	S
S	H	R	E	C	E	I	V	E	D	M	O
T	W	A	I	T	E	R	D	O	G	E	S

Activity #2

Role-play proper dining etiquette with your child. Pretend that you are eating in a restaurant, and demonstrate ways *not* to behave. Encourage your child to correct you, demonstrating how you *should* behave.

RULE #30

After your child eats, she should clean up after herself. This includes clearing the tables and making sure there isn't any trash left on the floor or around the eating area. It is important for your child to be responsible for cleaning up her trash no matter where she is and to be sure not to litter.

Activity #1

Read the scenarios below with your child. Have her rewrite the endings to show how each scenario should end.

SCENARIO 1: AT THE PARK

Justin and his friends are having lunch at the park. They get up to play soccer, leaving their trash behind on the table. A swift wind blows across the park, and the trash goes flying.

NEW ENDING:

_____

_____

_____

SCENARIO 2: AT THE FAST-FOOD RESTAURANT

Mary and her friends are enjoying their lunch at a fast-food restaurant. When they're finished, they go to the bathroom to wash their hands, and then they leave. A restaurant worker takes their trays full of trash and empties them in the trash can.

NEW ENDING:

_____

_____

_____

SCENARIO 3: AT THE FOOD COURT AT THE MALL

Katie, her mom, and her brothers are having lunch at the mall. Katie and her mom take their trays to the trash can. Her brothers do not. New customers, looking for a table, take the brothers' trays to the trash can themselves.

NEW ENDING:

_____

_____

_____

SCENARIO 4: AT THE CAFETERIA

Frank brings a lunch from home in a paper bag. When he's finished, he crumples up the bag and other trash—like his cupcake wrapper, napkin, banana peel, and milk carton—and leaves them in a neat pile on the table.

NEW ENDING:

_____

_____

_____

SCENARIO 5: AT HOME

Charisse and her family order Chinese take-out for dinner. The food comes in lots of cartons and containers. When Charisse is finished, she leaves the table to do homework. Her parents gather up the containers and throw them away.

NEW ENDING:

_____

_____

_____

Activity #2

Make a copy of this page for your child to take to school, to a restaurant, or to another place where he might make trash. Have him sketch the area in the first box to show what it looks like loaded with litter.

Now ask your child to draw the same scene, without the litter.

Ask your child to write a few sentences to describe and compare the place with litter and without litter. Encourage him to explain why cleaning up makes a place more enjoyable.

RULE #31

When people stay in a hotel room, it is appropriate to leave a tip on the pillow for the hotel workers who are responsible for cleaning the room. Two to three dollars per night is an appropriate amount, depending on the cost of the room.

Activity #1

In order to understand why tipping is important, it helps to recognize the various jobs that people do for others. Explain to your child that the people listed below do jobs that often require a tip for their services. Have your child draw a line to match the worker on the left with the job or service he or she does on the right.

1) waiter   a. cleans your room at a hotel

2) taxi driver   b. shows you things in an unfamiliar place

3) bellboy   c. serves food in a restaurant

4) maid   d. shows you to your seat and wipes it off

5) tour guide   e. carries your luggage at a hotel

6) usher at a ball game   f. takes you to your destination

The word *tip* is actually an acronym—a word that is made from the first letters of other words. So what words make up the acronym *tip: t-i-p*? Find out with your child by solving the puzzle below! The words below are found in the matched items on the previous page. Some letters have been filled in to help you.

W ____ (__) ____ S

C ____ (__) R ____ ____ ____

F (__) ____ ____

(__) A ____ D

(__) L ____ C ____

R ____ ____ (__) ____ ____ ____ ____ ____ T

T ____ ____ (__) ____ ____

B (__) ____ ____ B ____ ____

(__) ____ ____ V ____ ____

U (__) ____ ____ ____

Activity #2

Explain to your child that when people work for tips, they try hard to do a good job. If they do a good job, then their customers feel good about leaving a tip. Review the list of jobs in the previous activity. Ask your child what the worker could do to make people happy with his or her service. Then ask your child which of these jobs sound like fun. Have her write about one of the jobs on the lines below.

I think this job would be fun: _____ .

If I were a _____ , my job

responsibilities would include: _____

_____

_____ .

I know the money I would earn would depend on tips I receive from others. I would work hard to get good tips by:

_____

_____

_____ .

From now on, when I see other _____ ,

I will understand how hard they work to earn their tips! They must _____

_____

_____

_____

_____

_____

_____

_____

_____

_____

_____

_____

RULE #32

Your child should know the rules for riding on a school bus. She should always sit facing forward. She should never turn around to talk to other students, stick anything out of the windows, or get out of her seat. When she exits the bus, she should always thank the bus driver.

Activity #1

Does your child know how to behave on the school bus? Find out! Explain to her that behaving appropriately on a bus is necessary for safety. If the students behave well, then the driver can concentrate on driving rather than watching them on the bus. Read the behavior and actions in the list below. Ask your child to sort the activities on the chart to show which behaviors are appropriate and which are not.

read a book hang out the window stand up and stretch

fight or wrestle   whisper to a friend   do homework

switch seats   thank the driver   throw things to a friend

scream to get attention   face forward   sit quietly

THINGS WE CAN DO ON THE BUS	THINGS WE *CANNOT* DO ON THE BUS

Activity 2

Invite your child to read the story below. Afterward, talk about why the bus ride is called a "nightmare."

NIGHTMARE ON BUS #1313

It started out like any other bus ride. Everyone was quietly doing homework and softly talking to friends. Suddenly, Barbara let out a huge scream. Zach and Owen were fighting! Alicia told her friend Stacy to ignore the fight, but Stacy had to see what was going on. Alicia remained in her seat, but Stacy jumped up and ran to the back of the bus. Other kids joined her. Billy and Roger thought about trying to break up the fight, but they figured they'd only make things worse. Instead, they sat in their seats and faced forward. Olivia thought it would be best to get the bus driver's attention, so she threw an eraser at the driver's head. Luckily, Sam, who was reading a book at the front of the bus, caught the eraser before it could startle the bus driver. Oscar, who was sitting in the back of the bus, didn't know what to do. He was shocked when Barbara put her head out the window and started screaming some more, but he remained in his seat and tried to finish his homework. Vanessa also faced forward and tried to concentrate on editing her English composition. Suddenly, the bus swerved erratically, and all the kids who were standing fell to the floor. The bus driver pulled over and shook her head.

"I was too distracted by the fight," she later told the police. "I was watching the kids in the back of the bus to make sure they didn't hurt themselves, and I didn't realize how sharp the turn was. Luckily, no one was hurt."

This time.

Point out that although some kids on the bus behaved badly, a few kids behaved properly. Have your child list the kids' names below.

WHO BEHAVED PROPERLY ON THE BUS?	WHO BEHAVED BADLY ON THE BUS?
_____	_____
_____	_____
_____	_____
_____	_____
_____	_____

Now write the first letters of the names of the kids:

Kids Who Behaved Properly: _____

Kids Who Behaved Badly: _____

Unscramble the letters to reveal a word that describes each group of kids:

Kids who behaved properly are bus _____ .

Kids who behaved badly are bus _____

RULE #33

When your child goes on field trips, she will meet different people. When she is introduced to the people, she should make sure to remember their names. Then, when she is leaving, she should shake hands and thank them, mentioning their names as she does so.

Activity #1

Invite your child to play this memory game. You will need at least five other people to help you. These volunteers represent new people your child might meet, and you will assign them new names.

STEP 1

The game begins with you. Complete the chart on page 141. In the first column, list the people who will help you. In the second column, list the new names that you give them. For example, your neighbor, Mrs. Jones, might become Ms. Bennett, the school principal.

NAME OF FAMILY MEMBER OR FRIEND　　　　　**NEW NAME**

_____　　　　_____

_____　　　　_____

_____　　　　_____

_____　　　　_____

_____　　　　_____

_____　　　　_____

_____　　　　_____

_____　　　　_____

STEP 2

Cover up the new names in the second column with a sheet of paper.

STEP 3

Now, introduce your child to these "new" people with a sentence like "Nina, I'd like to introduce you to Ms. Bennett. Ms. Bennett is the new principal at the school." Observe how your child responds. Is she polite? Does she repeat the person's name?

STEP 4

After you've introduced your child to these "new" people, show her the list of names in the first column. Ask if she can recall the names you stated in your introductions. Tally how many names your child remembered.

STEP 5

Finally, share with your child the technique of recalling the names of new people she meets: repeating others' names out loud as they are introduced! Demonstrate by encouraging her to introduce you to someone new, and respond with a sentence like "Hello, Martin. It's so nice to meet you." If interest holds, you might play the memory game again, reminding your child to repeat the name of the person in the formal greeting. See if she remembers more names this time.

Activity #2

Help your child complete these greeting and leaving salutations. Read each scenario, and then have him write what he should say after the introduction. Also have him write what he should say upon leaving. To provide additional practice, role-play each scenario, letting him speak the words he has written.

SCENARIO 1: ON A FIELD TRIP TO A LOCAL PARK, YOUR TEACHER INTRODUCES THE PARK RANGER.

Teacher: Class, this is Miss Myers. She is a park ranger here at Colonial Park.

What should you say? _____

_____

What should you say when you leave? _____

_____

SCENARIO 2: ON A FIELD TRIP TO A MUSEUM, YOUR TEACHER INTRODUCES THE MUSEUM DIRECTOR.

Teacher: Everyone, this is Mr. Santos. He is the museum's director. He will show us around today.

What should you say? _____

_____

What should you say when you leave? _____

_____

SCENARIO 3: DURING CAREER DAY, YOUR TEACHER INTRODUCES A CLASS VISITOR.

Teacher: Class, this is Mrs. Patterson. She is here today to tell us about working for a newspaper.

What should you say? _____

_____

What should you say when you leave? _____

_____

SCENARIO 4: WHILE YOU'RE ON VACATION WITH YOUR PARENTS, THE TOUR GUIDE AT A HISTORICAL SITE INTRODUCES HIMSELF.

Tour guide: Hello, everyone! My name is Theo Smith. I will be taking you around Fort McHenry today.

What should you say? _____

_____

What should you say when you leave? _____

_____

SCENARIO 5: AT HOME, YOUR PARENTS INTRODUCE YOU TO NEW NEIGHBORS.

Parents: Toby, I want you to meet Mr. and Mrs. Nelson. They just moved in next door. They came from Florida.

What should you say? _____

_____

What should you say when you leave? _____

_____

RULE #34

Whenever your child is offered food, whether it is at a buffet or treats in class, he should never take more than his fair share. He shouldn't be greedy and try to get more, not only because it is wasteful, but also because it is disrespectful if he does not leave enough for others.

Activity #1

It's always tempting to take more than we should, especially if what is being offered is "free" or "all you can eat." See how well your child is able to control his appetite to overindulge when it comes to eating in public. Have him circle the number that best describes how often he engages in the behaviors listed, with 0 being never and 3 being always.

	NEVER			ALWAYS
1. At an all-you-can-eat buffet, I try every food I see, even if I might not like it.	0	1	2	3
2. At a buffet, I fill my plate so it is overflowing.	0	1	2	3

	NEVER			ALWAYS
3. At a buffet, I cut the line wherever there is food I like.	0	1	2	3
4. At a buffet, I grab food with my hands instead of using the utensils provided.	0	1	2	3
5. At a buffet, I take a lot of the food that I really like, even if I leave none for the people behind me.	0	1	2	3
6. When walking back from the buffet, I start eating the food that is on my plate.	0	1	2	3
7. If I return to the buffet for seconds, I put as much food as I can on my plate.	0	1	2	3
8. If desserts are offered at the buffet, I look for the biggest piece of cake, pie, or cookie.	0	1	2	3
9. When food is offered in class or at a party, I look for the biggest piece.	0	1	2	3
10. If two pieces of food are left in a dish, I take both pieces so no pieces are left.	0	1	2	3

CHECK YOUR SCORE!

If you scored 0–6 You're a diner extraordinaire! You know not to overdo it at the buffet, and you are considerate to the other diners.

If you scored 7–14 You're a dandy diner! Sometimes you may overdo it at the buffet line, especially if the buffet serves a food you really like. For the most part, though, you know your limits and you don't try to take more than you can eat.

If you scored 15–22 You're a mucho muncher! You tend to take more food than you can eat. You usually take the last piece of food or the biggest piece. Try not to go back for seconds— and leave the best and biggest pieces for your friends!

If you scored 23–30 You're a gluttonous gobbler! Your plate is always overflowing with food, even though you know you can't eat it all. In fact, you'll go back for seconds, even if you're full! You tend to look for the biggest and best piece that the buffet or platter has to offer. You need to curtail your gobbling hobby and enjoy your food in smaller portions. Try to be more generous to the diners around you.

Activity #2

Does your child know the word for eating too much? Help her solve this puzzle to find out. Work with her to complete each sentence with the correct word from the box. The word for eating to excess will appear in the boxes that run down the page.

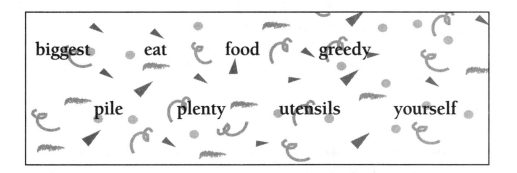

You should not take the _____ piece on the plate.

You should not _____ your food so it overflows your plate.

You should not take the last piece for _____ .

You should use the _____ at the buffet table, not your hands.

You should not _____ from your plate while you are walking.

It is never polite to take too much _____ at a buffet.

You should leave _____ of food for others.

You should not be _____ at a buffet table.

___ ___ ☐ ___ ___ ___ ___ ___

___ ___ ☐ ___

___ ___ ☐ ___ ___ ___ ___ ___

___ ☐ ___ ___ ___ ___ ___ ___ ___

___ ___ ☐ ___

___ ___ ☐ ___ ___

___ ___ ___ ☐ ___ ___ ___

___ ___ ___ ___ ___ ☐ ___

RULE #35

In school, on a field trip, at home, or out with friends or family, if someone drops something near her, your child should pick it up and hand it back. Even if the person is closer to the object, it is only polite to make the gesture of bending down to retrieve the item.

Activity #1

What does your child do when she notices that someone has dropped something? Find out! Invite her to circle what she might do in each situation below. Then check her score.

1. The person who sits next to you in class drops his pencil. You:
   a) pick it up for him.
   b) pick it up and keep it.
   c) leave it on the floor.

2. Your teacher accidentally knocks over a stack of papers. You are nearby, so you:
   a) help the teacher pick up the papers.
   b) step on a sheet of paper and continue walking.
   c) leave the papers on the floor.

3. While walking down the hallway at school, a student passes you and drops a book. You:

   a) take a moment to pick it up.

   b) kick it across the hall.

   c) ignore it.

4. While running across the playground at recess with your friends, you see something fall out of a friend's pocket. You stop running and:

   a) pick it up and return it to your friend.

   b) pick it up and pretend that you dropped it.

   c) leave it where it fell.

5. A person you don't know in the cafeteria drops a tray of food. You are nearby, so you:

   a) help the student pick up the dropped tray and food.

   b) step on a dropped cookie.

   c) ignore the commotion and meet your friends.

6. At home, the person cooking dinner drops a stirring spoon while you are doing homework. You:

   a) pick it up, rinse it off, and hand it back to the cook.

   b) laugh and call the cook a klutz.

   c) continue doing your homework without looking up.

7. At home, a younger sibling drops a favorite toy. You:

   a) rush over and pick it up before he starts to cry.

   b) yell at him and tell him to be more careful.

   c) pretend you didn't notice.

8. At the store, you see someone drop a dollar bill. You:

   a) pick it up and return it to its owner.

   b) pick it up and keep it for yourself.

   c) pretend you don't see it.

9. At the movie theater, you see someone drop her ticket. You:

   a) pick it up and tell the person that she dropped the ticket.

   b) pick it up and give it to a friend.

   c) leave it; it's not your problem.

10. At the library, someone drops a big stack of books. You:

   a) rush to help pick up the books.

   b) point out the mishap to your friends and laugh.

   c) roll your eyes at the noise and continue to work.

CHECK YOUR SCORE!

If you circled mostly As:

Wonderful! You are extremely helpful and considerate of others, and you usually pick up an object that someone has dropped. Keep up the good work!

If you circled mostly Bs:

Yikes! You're not very helpful at all. In fact, sometimes you even hurt others by your actions. Try to remember that just because people drop something doesn't mean they don't need or want it. Imagine how you would feel if you dropped something and someone else took it! The saying "Finders keepers, losers weepers" is not a nice way to go through life. Try to be more considerate when people drop things.

If you circled mostly Cs:

Bummer! Although you might not contribute anything negative to the situation, you certainly don't help out. Ignoring an object that has been dropped is not better than picking it up and keeping it for yourself. You need to start thinking of others instead of yourself and offer your help if someone has dropped something. You can do it!

Activity #2

Challenge your child to help each person in the left column "pick up" the object that he or she has dropped. Tell your child to write the letter of the dropped object on the line next to the person who dropped it. If all the items have been correctly "picked up" and given to the correct owner, what the owners say will appear in the column of letters your child writes.

_____ a mail carrier   a) a grocery list

_____ a small child on a cold day   y) a purse

_____ someone at the grocery store   k) a library card

_____ the school principal   o) an airplane ticket

_____ someone at the library   t) a letter

_____ a woman at a restaurant   u) keys

_____ a person at an airport   h) a mitten

_____ someone in a parking lot   n) a pen

RULE #36

If your child approaches a door and someone is close behind, he should hold the door. If the door opens by pulling, he should pull it open, stand to the side, and allow the other person to pass through first; then your child can walk through. If the door opens by pushing, he should hold the door after he passes through.

Activity #1

How often do people hold the door open for each other? Who holds the door open more often—kids or adults? Work with your child to find out! Choose a public place where many people go in and out of a door. Observe how often people hold the door open for each other and how often they do not. Color in squares on the bar graph to record your observations.

KIDS WHO HOLD THE DOOR OPEN

KIDS WHO DO _NOT_ HOLD THE DOOR OPEN

ADULTS WHO HOLD THE DOOR OPEN

ADULTS WHO DO _NOT_ HOLD THE DOOR OPEN

Now interpret your results!

Who held the door open most often? _____

Who held the door open less frequently? _____

What conclusions can you draw from your observations? _____

_____

What should you do when you approach a door?_____

_____

_____

_____

_____

_____

_____

_____

Activity #2

The limericks below tell the silly stories of silly people and their door-holding experiences. Take turns reading the limericks out loud with your child. Embedded within the limericks is a secret message. After reading the limericks, follow the directions to crack the code.

LIMERICK #1

There once was a man named All-Bright,

Who tried hard to be so polite.

He held open the door,

Ten went through, then ten more!

So he held the door open all night.

LIMERICK #2

There once was a girl from the shore,

Who started to go through a door.

She pushed the door open,

And let a whole crowd in,

And not once did she wonder, "What for?"

LIMERICK #3

There once were two sisters from Spain,

Who thought being polite was a pain.

They pushed through the door,

Squeezed and squished until sore—

And between them they had not one brain.

LIMERICK #4

There once were two brothers from Kreetch,

Who acted polite as a peach.

"First you!" said one brother.

"No, you!" said the other,

As they held the door open for each.

CRACK THE CODE!

- ▸ The first number is the limerick.
- ▸ The second number is the line.
- ▸ The third number is the word.

Write the words for each set of numbers on the lines to reveal the secret message.

1-2-5	3-2-4	2-2-3	4-5-8
_____	_____	_____	_____

4-4-5	2-3-5	3-3-4	1-3-5
_____	_____	_____	_____!

RULE #37

If someone bumps into your child, she should say "Excuse me" even if it was not her fault.

Activity #1

Ask your child to read the situations below. Have her circle **true** or **false** to show when it is appropriate to say "Excuse me." Count up all the trues and check her score.

1. You should say "Excuse me" when you bump into someone.   True   False

2. You should say "Excuse me" when someone bumps into you.   True   False

3. You should say "Excuse me" if you step on someone's foot on the bus.   True   False

4. You should say "Excuse me" if someone steps on your foot on the bus.   True   False

5. You should say "Excuse me" if you knock someone's pencil off the desk.　　　　　　　　True　　　　　False

6. You should say "Excuse me" if someone knocks your pencil off your desk.　　　　　　True　　　　　False

7. You should say "Excuse me" if you spill a drink on someone.　　　　　　　　　　　True　　　　　False

8. You should say "Excuse me" if someone spills a drink on you.　　　　　　　　　　True　　　　　False

9. You should say "Excuse me" if you trip on someone's foot.　　　　　　　　　　True　　　　　False

10. You should say "Excuse me" if someone trips on your foot.　　　　　　　　　　True　　　　　False

CHECK YOUR SCORE!

If you circled mostly trues: You're excused! You know that it's always best to say "Excuse me," rather than to blame someone else for a bump or a push or a trip or a spill. You don't get offended easily, and you feel confident enough to take the blame, even if it isn't your fault.

If you circled mostly true on the odd numbers, but mostly false on the even numbers: You're not excused! You know that you should say "Excuse me" if it is your fault, but you have a hard time saying the words if it is someone else's fault. It doesn't matter whose fault it is! You will always be in the right if you say "Excuse me." Try to be more "excusing" and less "accusing."

If you circled mostly falses: No more excuses! You have a difficult time admitting when you might be in the wrong. You need to gain more confidence and not let silly things like bumps and trips affect you. The next time bumping occurs, try to say "Excuse me." You'll find that the tension will go away with these two simple words. So no more excuses! Excuse yourself!

Activity #2

Your child might need to work on saying "Excuse me" during accidental physical contacts, like bumping or tripping. Talk with him about the importance of saying "Excuse me" even if the bump is not his fault. Then encourage him to keep a log of bumping or other accidental contacts. Have him describe the incident and note if he said "Excuse me." In the last column, instruct him to write down the outcome of the incident. Every few days, review the log, and help your child realize that when he said "Excuse me," no further altercation usually occurred.

DATE	WHAT HAPPENED?	DID YOU SAY "EXCUSE ME"?	WHAT WAS THE OUTCOME?

RULE #38

When your child is on a field trip with his class, there will be no talking upon entering a building. The students should enter the building quietly so that no one even notices that they are there. This rule applies to entering any place where people are gathered, whether it is the movies, a church, a theater, or any other venue.

Activity #1

Tell your child to fill in the missing letters below to show that he knows what to do when entering a building. A secret message will be revealed in the diagonal box.

When you enter a theater, you should: E QUIET!
When you enter a restaurant, you should: B   QUIET!
When you enter a museum, you should: B E   UIET!
When you enter an art gallery, you should: B E Q   IET!
When you enter a library, you should: B E QU   ET!
When you enter an office building, you should: B E QUI   T!
When you enter a national monument, you should: B E QUIE   !

Think of other buildings that you enter, either on a field trip, with your friends, or with your family. Complete each sentence on the next page with the names of other buildings that you should enter quietly.

I should be quiet when I enter _____.

I should be quiet when I enter _____.

I should be quiet when I enter _____.

Activity #2

Read the short story below with your child. Discuss the disruptive behavior of the kids and the negative reactions of the adults. Work with your child to rewrite the story to show how the kids *should* behave and how the adults react to that behavior. You might point out the cause and effect of their actions: Good behavior results in good reactions; bad behavior results in bad reactions.

A DAY AT THE MUSEUM

Mr. Evans's class was out of control. The students were supposed to be on a pleasant field trip to a local museum. The bus ride over had been bad enough, with kids running up and down the bus aisles and throwing things and talking loudly. Mr. Evans thought the kids would get it out of their system—when they entered the museum, they would be quiet.

Hardly! The class entered the museum divided into small groups of friends, each one talking louder than the next. A few kids remained outside, and they only straggled in when Mr. Evans went to get them. Small groups broke off from the class to run to exhibits that interested them, talking loudly and pointing at things. Several adults nearby shook their heads and quickly moved on to another room. A family with small children tried to hush their children, who had begun to cry at the unexpected noise. The museum director rushed to Mr. Evans and insisted that he get his class under control or they would have to leave. Eventually, Mr. Evans was able to round up his students and quiet them down. However, the guide who was supposed to lead them through the museum decided to take another class that was better behaved. Mr. Evans and his class had to venture through the museum on their own, which took much longer and required them to cut their lunch short.

How should Mr. Evans's students have behaved? How would the other people at the museum have reacted to this different behavior? Rewrite the story!

_____

_____

_____

_____

_____

_____

_____

_____

_____

RULE #39

If your child's class is on a field trip, it is a good idea to compliment something about the place they are visiting. For example, if visiting someone's home, it would be a nice gesture for your child to admire the curtains. People are always self-conscious when they have guests visit their home, so she should learn to make them feel at ease. When visiting other places, such as a museum or theater, she could tell the guide how beautiful the architecture is.

Activity #1

Does your child understand what it means to "compliment" someone? Find out! Have her read each scenario below and circle the person that is offering a compliment.

1. Curtis and Michelle are visiting Curtis's grandmother. Curtis tells his grandmother how much he likes her flower garden. Michelle asks Curtis's grandmother if they can watch TV.

    Who is offering a compliment?   Curtis   Michelle

2. Tina and Orlando are visiting their aunt and uncle. Orlando points out how good the house smells—full of the scent of fresh-baked cookies. Tina asks when the cookies will be ready.

    Who is offering a compliment?   Tina   Orlando

3. Marta and her friends have been invited to see a play at an old theater. Marta's friends giggle as they go to their seats. Marta points out how cool the curtains look, all gold and shimmery.

    Who is offering a compliment?   Marta   Marta's friends

4. Frances and Kelvin enter the visitors' center of a national monument. Kelvin wants to know where the bathroom is. Frances comments that she loves the old feel of the place.

    Who is offering a compliment?   Frances   Kelvin

5. It is orientation day at the new high school. Turner and Otto both enter the school building. Turner points out the ugly color of the hallway. Otto points out how new and clean everything looks.

    Who is offering a compliment?   Turner   Otto

6. Ryan and Peter have been invited to a baseball game. Ryan exclaims at how big and green the field looks. Peter wants to know when they can get hot dogs.

    Who is offering a compliment?   Ryan   Peter

7. Wanda and Tameeka have entered the new store at the mall. Wanda comments on how small the store is. Tameeka comments on the cool display of clothes.

    Who is offering a compliment?   Wanda   Tameeka

8. Thomas and Andrew have been dropped off at summer camp. As they stare around their cabin, Thomas asks the camp counselor why the cabin smells like a wet dog. Andrew tells the camp counselor that he loves the rustic feel of the cabin.

    Who is offering a compliment?   Thomas   Andrew

9. Beth and Gina are visiting the new home of a friend, Kezia. Beth says that she loves the way Kezia has arranged the furniture in her new room. Gina tells Kezia that she would have more space if she moved her bed under the window.

    Who is offering a compliment?   Beth   Gina

10. Mateo and Linda decide to visit their teacher, who lives in the same neighborhood. Mateo asks the teacher why he doesn't have any video games. Linda tells the teacher that she really likes his shelves full of books.

    Who is offering a compliment?   Mateo   Linda

11. Maya and Eric are trying out a new restaurant with their families. Maya tells the waiter that the tables are too close together. Eric states that he thinks the restaurant is cozy.

    Who is offering a compliment?   Maya   Eric

Why is it important to offer compliments when you are visiting? Write the first letter of the names of the kids you circled, in order. If you circled the correct names, the answer will be revealed!

When you compliment the places you visit, you make other people feel:

____ ____ ____ ____ ____ ____ ____ ____ ____ ____ ____ !

Activity #2

Ask your child to think of the people and places he visits. It can be a place visited during a field trip or an outing with the family, or the home of a family member or friend. Ask your child to write down the place, then to add something that he could compliment about the place.

PLACE TO VISIT	COMPLIMENT
1. _____	_____
2. _____	_____

PLACE TO VISIT	**COMPLIMENT**
3. _____	_____
4. _____	_____
5. _____	_____
6. _____	_____
7. _____	_____
8. _____	_____
9. _____	_____
10. _____	_____
11. _____	_____
12. _____	_____
13. _____	_____
14. _____	_____
15. _____	_____
16. _____	_____

RULE #40

During a school assembly, your child should not speak or look around to try to get the attention of his friends. Each class must uphold an image that shows they have respect for themselves and others.

Activity #1

The actions listed below tell what kids should do when going to a school assembly. The actions, though, are out of order. Help your child rewrite the actions in the correct order on page 170.

Walk to the auditorium.

Remain quiet throughout the assembly.

Place your hands in your lap

Get up from your seat in class.

File into the designated rows.

Line up inside the classroom.

Face forward in your seat.

Sit down quietly.

THE PROCEDURE WE SHOULD FOLLOW
WHEN WE GO TO A SCHOOL ASSEMBLY

1. _____

2. _____

3. _____

4. _____

5. _____

6. _____

7. _____

8. _____

Have your child write a silly sentence to help him remember the proper procedure for school assemblies. Have him use the first letter of each step to create the sentence. For example:

Gary Loony Was Falling Sideways, Feeling Purple Rabbits.

_____

_____

Activity #2

A school assembly can have many distractions. What should your child do in such distracting circumstances? Have her circle the answers below that illustrate the best behavior she should strive for.

1) If someone calls your name, you should:
   a) not respond
   b) turn around and wave
   c) say, "Shh!"

2) If someone tosses a paper ball at your head, you should:
   u) throw it back
   v) tell the teacher
   w) ignore it

3) If someone makes a loud, silly noise, you should:
   d) giggle quietly
   e) try to remain silent
   f) make a noise, too

4) If two kids behind you are talking loudly, you should:
   r) turn around and glare
   s) face forward
   t) throw something at them

5) If someone yells out a joke and the other students start to clap and cheer, you should:
   m) clap along with them
   n) whistle loudly
   o) keep your hands in your lap

6) While the assembly presenters are speaking, you should:
   m) remain quiet and listen
   n) remain quiet and read
   o) talk softly to your friend

7) When leaving the assembly, you should:
   c) leave as quickly as possible
   d) finally wave to your friends
   e) leave quietly

Did you choose the correct answers? Find out! Write the letters of your answers on the lines below, in order. If your answers are correct, the letters will spell a word that describes your assembly behavior.

____ ____ ____ ____ ____ ____ ____ !

RULE #41

Your child should learn to answer the phone at home in an appropriate manner.

Activity #1

Establish your own family etiquette for answering the phone at home. You'll want to teach your child how to answer the phone with a polite greeting, how to identify herself, how to identify who is calling, how to put people on hold, how to pass the phone to another person, and how to conclude a call. Make a checklist with your child that you can leave by the phone, reminding her of the steps to take while on the phone, and how to respond politely to the caller.

Activity #2

When someone calls, the person he or she is asking for might not be home. Review with your child how to politely take a message. Role-play these words with your child:

Your Child: Hello, this is the _____ residence.
Caller (You): May I speak to _____?
Your Child: I'm sorry, she/he is not here right now.
Would you like to leave a message?

—OR—

Your Child: I'm sorry, she/he cannot come to the phone right now. Would you like to leave a message?

(Note: You might prefer the latter response so the caller will not think that your child is home alone.)

Caller: Yes, I would like to leave a message.

Your Child: Okay, may I have your name and number?

Caller: (Provide information for your child to write down.)

Your Child: (Have your child repeat the information he or she has written down to make sure it is correct.)

Caller: Yes, that's right.

Your Child: I will make sure she/he gets the message. Good-bye.

Caller: Thank you. Good-bye.

To further assist your child with taking phone messages, you might keep a message pad or message sheets near the phone. We've provided one here that you can copy for that purpose. Make sure you have a pen near the phone, too!

TAKE A MESSAGE!

Who called? _____

Whom did the caller ask for? _____

What's the caller's phone number? _____

What's the message? _____

_____

_____

_____

What day did she/he call? _____

What time did she/he call? _____

Should I call back? Yes _____ No_____

RULE #42

Teaching your child to say thank you when others do something for him is important at home and in school. When your child's class returns from a trip, he should shake hands with the teacher and every chaperone. Your child should thank them for taking the class on the trip and let them know that he appreciates having the opportunity to go.

Activity #1

Have your child read about each field trip on the next three pages. Then work with him to write dialogue showing how the students on the field trip should have responded. Role-play these scenes with him to reinforce the habit of thanking people who have helped the class.

THE NATIONAL ZOO

Mr. Myers's class spent a day at the National Zoo in Washington, D.C. Because the zoo is large and sprawling, many parents and family members were enlisted to chaperone. When the class returned to school, the kids ran off the bus and into the school building. The chaperones looked around, bewildered, and then realized that their duty was done. They slowly walked to the parking lot, got into their cars, and drove away.

WHAT SHOULD THE KIDS IN MR. MYERS'S CLASS HAVE DONE?

Student: _____

Chaperone: _____

Student: _____

Chaperone: _____

Student: _____

THE CONCERT HALL

Miss Tirado took her students to a concert hall to share with them her love of classical music. Several parent volunteers, along with a few teacher's aides, enjoyed the concert as well. In fact, the field trip would not have been possible without the help of the parents and teacher's aides as chaperones. After the concert, the class, chaperones, and Miss Tirado went out for pizza. The kids all sat at one table, and the chaperones sat at another.

WHAT SHOULD THE KIDS IN MISS TIRADO'S CLASS HAVE DONE?

Student: _____

Chaperone: _____

Student: _____

Chaperone: _____

Student: _____

THE OUTDOOR CAMP

Every year, the entire sixth grade at Washington Middle School spent a week at an outdoor camp. Although chaperones were not needed, student volunteers from the local high school attended the camp as camp counselors. The student volunteers were not paid, and when they returned to their own school, they had a lot of work to make up. The student volunteers felt the experience was worth it—they liked helping the sixth graders complete projects and activities. However, when the week ended, the sixth graders boarded the bus and headed home with hardly a backward glance.

WHAT SHOULD THE SIXTH GRADERS HAVE DONE?

Student: _____

Chaperone: _____

Student: _____

Chaperone: _____

Student: _____

Activity #2

Mention to your child that she needs to thank people who frequently help her. Talk with her about these people and the things they do. Have her write the people's names in the chart below, as well as a brief sentence that explains how that person helps her. For example, perhaps an older sibling helps her with math homework, or a grandparent watches her while you work late, or a neighbor teaches her about the plants in his garden. Let your child fill in the chart each time someone offers help. Review with her that we should always thank the people who help us.

WHO HELPS YOU?	WHAT DOES HE OR SHE DO?	DO YOU SAY "THANK YOU"?
1. _____	_____	_____
2. _____	_____	_____
3. _____	_____	_____
4. _____	_____	_____
5. _____	_____	_____
6. _____	_____	_____
7. _____	_____	_____

WHO HELPS YOU?	WHAT DOES HE OR SHE DO?	DO YOU SAY "THANK YOU"?
8. _____	_____	_____
9. _____	_____	_____
10. _____	_____	_____
11. _____	_____	_____
12. _____	_____	_____
13. _____	_____	_____
14. _____	_____	_____
15. _____	_____	_____
16. _____	_____	_____

RULE #43

When your child is out with you or your family, or on field trips with her class, and has to use escalators, she should stand to the right. That will give other people who are in a hurry the option of walking up the left-hand side of the escalator. When entering an elevator, the subway, or a doorway, your child should wait for others to exit first.

Activity #1

Your child might not have everyday exposure to escalators, subways, trains, and elevators, but it doesn't hurt to know how to be polite and respectful when the time does come! Read the situations below. Have your child answer the question by circling **Yes** or **No**. Then help her explain the polite way to behave in each situation.

1. You are standing in the lobby of a hotel, waiting for the elevator. The elevator doors open, and you rush inside, forcing the people inside the elevator to push by you. You've been waiting a long time, after all.

   Is this the correct way to enter an elevator?   **Yes**   **No**

If you circled **No**, what is the polite way?

_____

_____

_____

2. You are riding up an escalator with a friend. Both of you stand on the same step, with your hands resting gently on the rails. You stand on the right side, and your friend stands on the left side. After all, you don't want to get separated when you get to the top.

Is this the correct way to ride on an escalator?   **Yes**   **No**

If you circled **No**, what is the polite way?

_____

_____

_____

3. You are waiting on a train or subway platform. The train or subway appears, and the doors slide open. You rush inside, nudging the people who are trying to get out. After all, you don't want to miss the train.

Is this the correct way to enter a train or subway?   **Yes**   **No**

If you circled **No**, what is the polite way?

_____

_____

_____

4. You are riding on a train or subway. Your stop is coming up, and a line of people is starting to form at the door. You nudge your way to the front of the line
and wait in front of the door. After all, you don't want to miss your stop.

Is this the correct way to exit a train or subway?   **Yes**   **No**

If you circled **No**, what is the polite way?

_____

_____

_____

5. The movie is over, and everyone in the theater heads for the exit. You hurry
forward and push through, even though an usher is trying to get in to start
cleaning the aisles. After all, your ride is waiting outside.

Is this the correct way to go through a doorway   **Yes**   **No**
when someone is coming the other way?

If you circled **No**, what is the polite way?

_____

_____

_____

Activity #2

Ask your child how to apply Rule #43 to her everyday life. Would she be able to use the basic principles of the rule in any of the following situations?

▸ On the playground?
▸ In the school cafeteria?
▸ Walking into school at the start of the day?
▸ Leaving school at the end of the day?
▸ Changing classrooms for different subjects?
▸ Running an errand for the teacher?
▸ Participating in a fire drill?

RULE #44

Discuss with your child the basic rules for behavior in school. He should understand what the teacher expects when the class needs to line up, how to proceed as a class to a destination, and the rules for maintaining quiet when necessary.

Activity #1

Often we are given rules without understanding their purpose. Lining up and remaining quiet might seem like a strict and unnecessary rule—until your child understands why it is important. Read with him the reasons below. Have him circle **True** if the statement is true or **False** if the statement is false.

1. Lining up shows that you don't know how to follow directions.   **True**   **False**

2. Lining up shows that you are not able to be organized.   **True**   **False**

3. Lining up shows that you don't know what is expected of you.   **True**   **False**

4. Walking in one or two lines down the hall shows that you have no idea where you are going.   **True**   **False**

5. Walking in one or two lines down the hall shows that you have absolutely no respect for rules.   **True**   **False**

6. Walking quietly down the hall shows that you do not respect others or the lessons going on in their classes.   **True**   **False**

7. Walking quietly and in a line shows that you do not have respect for yourself or your teacher.   **True**   **False**

8. Walking quietly and in a line demonstrates that you do not know the appropriate behavior for moving through the school.   **True**   **False**

Now work with your child to rewrite all the **False** statements so they are true. (Hint! Every statement above is false!)

1. _____

_____

2. _____

_____

3. _____

_____

4. _____

_____

5. _____

_____

6. _____

_____

7. _____

_____

8. _____

_____

Activity #2

Sing the song "The Ants Go Marching One by One" with your child. Ask her to write new lyrics for the song, describing walking one by one at school. The verses have been started below to jump-start her rhymes and imagination. Suggest that she sing the new words to herself in class the next time the students have to line up. She could even share the new lyrics with her classmates to further motivate them. But make sure she remembers that there should *not* be singing when silence is required!

Our class is marching one by one. Hurrah! Hurrah!
Our class is marching one by one. Hurrah! Hurrah!
Our class is marching one by one,

_____

_____

Our class is marching single file. Hurrah! Hurrah!
Our class is marching single file. Hurrah! Hurrah!
Our class is marching single file,

_____

_____

Our class is marching quietly. Hurrah! Hurrah!
Our class is marching quietly. Hurrah! Hurrah!
Our class is marching quietly,

_____

_____

Now try your own verse!

_____

_____

_____

_____

_____

RULE #45

Your child should know never to cut in line. If someone cuts in front of her, she should inform the teacher, who will handle the situation. By fussing with someone who has cut in line, your child could get in trouble as well. Students need to handle all disputes with other classmates in the same manner—by going to the teacher.

Activity #1

While it may seem difficult at times, it is sometimes better for kids to let an adult know when something is wrong than to take care of the situation themselves. Informing someone in charge protects not only themselves but other kids in school. See if your child knows the right thing to do in each situation below.

SCENARIO 1

Daniel and José get in a shoving match during lunch. Elijah tries to break them up, getting in between and shoving back. Scott runs to get a teacher.

Who did the right thing—Elijah or Scott?

SCENARIO 2

Antonio and Erica watch as Melissa steals an eraser from a classmate's desk. Antonio confronts Melissa, telling her that what she did isn't right and she should put the eraser back. Erica quietly tells the teacher what happened.

Who did the right thing—Antonio or Erica?

SCENARIO 3

Mario and Samuel are walking down the hall with their class. Suddenly, both Mario and Samuel fall. Mario knows that someone tripped them, and he confronts the suspects. Samuel decides instead to explain to the teacher what happened when she asks if they are okay.

Who did the right thing—Mario or Samuel?

SCENARIO 4

During recess, Enrique and Kelsey both notice a group of kids picking on a new kid in school. Kelsey goes over to stop the bullying. Enrique decides to alert a teacher.

Who did the right thing—Enrique or Kelsey?

SCENARIO 5

Mrs. Johnson's class is watching a movie. Two kids in the back of the room are telling jokes and giggling. Sharon turns around and hits one of them so they'll be quiet. Deena quietly gets up and explains what is happening to the teacher.

Who did the right thing—Sharon or Deena?

Discuss your child's answers with her and why or why not these might have been difficult decisions for them to make.

Activity #2

Encourage your child to keep a log of situations in which he confronted a classmate or wanted to confront a classmate. Have him briefly describe the situation below and then explain how he resolved the conflict. Encourage him to decide if this was the appropriate action to take, and discuss the reasons with him.

DATE	WHAT HAPPENED?	WHAT DID YOU DO?	WAS THIS THE RIGHT ACTION TO TAKE? EXPLAIN.

RULE #46

When your child goes to a movie theater, he should not talk at all during the film. He should not put his feet on the chair in front of him. He should open any food packages before the movie begins; trying to open a bag of candy during a movie is very annoying to others. He should eat any snacks as quietly as possible. It is also very rude to leave a cell phone or beeper on during a movie.

Activity #1

Which behaviors are acceptable in a movie theater and which are not? Have your child read the behaviors below. Then have him write the proper behaviors in the movie screen on page 193.

Talking loudly   Talking on a cell phone   Checking beeper
Sitting quietly   Feet on chair   Cell phone off
Feet on floor   Whispering and giggling   Opening candy
Candy already opened   Facing forward   Asking questions
Beeper off   Turning around in seat   Quietly eating popcorn

Review the behaviors your child listed—as well as those he did not list. Talk about why each behavior is appropriate or inappropriate for a movie theater.

Activity #2

Invite your child to complete each sentence below with a word from the box. Then help her find the words in the word-find puzzle. The words appear across, down, and diagonally.

beeper	candy	cell phone	chair	eat

face	feet	play	proper	quietly

rude	video	whisper	wrapper

a. When eating _____ , it is best to open the _____ before the movie.

b. You should always turn off your _____ and your _____ _____ when inside a movie theater.

c. It is best to keep your _____ off the _____ in front of you.

d. You should not _____ a _____ game during a movie.

e. The polite way to _____ during a movie is very _____.

f. You can only watch a movie if you _____ forward, so do not turn around.

g. Even a _____ can be loud in a movie theater. Absolutely no talking.

h. It is _____ not to follow the _____ behavior in a movie theater.

C	E	L	L	P	H	O	N	E
A	F	A	C	E	F	O	P	W
N	M	O	W	V	E	I	L	R
D	E	E	H	D	E	T	A	A
Y	Q	U	I	E	T	L	Y	P
I	Q	V	S	R	U	D	E	P
P	R	O	P	E	R	U	A	E
E	B	E	E	P	E	R	T	R
T	T	E	R	C	H	A	I	R

Now write the letters you did not use, in order, on the lines below to complete this sentence:

Practicing proper behavior in a movie theater shows that you have good

___ ___ ___ ___ ___

___ ___ ___ ___ ___ ___ ___ ___ ___!

RULE #47

Your child should not bring Doritos into her school building.

Activity #1

This might seem like a silly rule—and that's just the point! Even though the rule does have some merit (Doritos can turn your fingers orange and might cause disputes during class), for the most part the rule is silly and goofy. Does your child feel that any rules at school are silly or goofy, like this Doritos rule? Have her list rules that her class follows, as well as the reasons for those rules. Then have her draw a star beside any rule that she thinks is silly. You might also discuss rules you follow at home.

CLASS OR SCHOOL RULES   **PURPOSE**

1. _____   _____

2. _____   _____

3. _____   _____

4. _____   _____

5. _____   _____

Activity #2

Brainstorm with your child rules that sound as silly as the Doritos rule. Have him write down the rule and then explain its purpose. Let him be creative and write down any silly rule that comes to mind. You might suggest that he share the rules with his teacher. You never know—maybe the teacher will add the rule to the class list!

MY SILLY RULES　　　　　　**PURPOSE**

a. _____　　_____

b. _____　　_____

c. _____　　_____

d. _____　　_____

e. _____　　_____

RULE #48

If any child in school is bothering your child, he should let the teacher know. The teacher is there to look after and protect your child and should not let anyone in the school bully your child or make him feel uncomfortable. Your child should not take matters into his own hands; he should let the teacher deal with the bully.

Activity #1

Being bullied is probably one of the worst childhood experiences. Even adults often must deal with bullies, such as neighbors or coworkers. Adults usually feel powerful enough to defend themselves. Children, however, usually feel incapable of defending themselves. Instead, their self-esteem plummets, and they feel they have no recourse but to put up with being bullied. Have your child answer the questions below to tell about a time when he was bullied, either at school, on the playground, in the neighborhood, or perhaps even at home. Talk with him about the experience.

Write about a time when someone bullied you. _____

_____

_____

_____

How did you feel? _____

_____

_____

_____

What did you do? _____

_____

_____

_____

Do you think you did the right thing? Why or why not? _____

_____

_____

_____

Activity #2

Sometimes kids aren't sure whom to turn to when someone bullies them. Although it might seem like tattling, getting an adult or an older sibling or friend involved is often the best solution. It proves to your child that someone is in her corner, which reinforces her self-esteem. And because someone older will seem intimidating to the bully, the bullying usually stops. Help your child recognize whom she can turn to when being bullied by matching the situation with a potential ally.

IF SOMEONE BULLIES YOU . . .	YOU CAN TURN TO:
1. on the playground	b) your gym teacher
2. in class	d) a parent or older relative
3. in the school hallway	e) a lifeguard
4. in the neighborhood	l) a lunchroom monitor
5. at the neighborhood pool	m) the playground monitor
6. in your family	o) your teacher
7. at lunch	r) a teacher or other school adult
8. at the library	s) a security guard
9. in gym class	t) an older sibling, relative, or neighbor
10. at the mall	u) the librarian

Now write the letters that you matched to each number to complete the rhyme below. Say the rhyme to yourself and remember it the next time you get bullied!

_____ _____ _____ _____ i_____ _____ a_____ _____
  9   8   7   7   5   10   3   5

a _____ _____ _____ _____ !
   9   2   3   5

_____ h_____ w _____ h_____ _____ _____ _____ _____ _____
10   2   4   5   1   2   8   4

_____ h_____ _____ _____ _____ _____ !
  4   5   6   2   2   3!

RULE #49

Your child should stand up for what she believes in. She shouldn't take no for an answer if her heart and mind are leading her in a direction that she feels strongly about.

Activity #1

How often does your child take the difficult path and stand up for what she believes in? How often does she simply take the easy way out? Invite her to take this test to find out. In addition, you will learn what types of things are important to her. Have your child choose **Always**, **Sometimes**, or **Never**.

1. You feel more strongly about one candidate for class president than the other, but all your friends are voting for the popular choice. You vote for your choice, no matter what. **Always** **Sometimes** **Never**

2. You feel that a class punishment is unfair. You explain to your teacher how you feel. **Always** **Sometimes** **Never**

3. Kids are ignoring the recycling trash bin. You know it is better to recycle, and you point out what the kids should be doing. **Always   Sometimes   Never**

4. You receive a bad grade on a report. Your teacher feels that you copied your information from a book instead of using your own words. You defend your work. **Always   Sometimes   Never**

5. A friend gets in trouble, but you know it is really your fault. You stick up for your friend and take responsibility. **Always   Sometimes   Never**

6. The school has decided to cancel a basketball game with a rival school for fear that fights will break out. You feel strongly that the basketball game should go on, and you rally others to your point of view. **Always   Sometimes   Never**

7. Your teacher decides that the class is not responsible enough to take a field trip to a nearby museum. You feel that the class is ready, so you defend your class. **Always   Sometimes   Never**

8. You really want a dog, but your parents say no. You plead your case, explaining all the ways in which a dog will help you learn responsibility. **Always   Sometimes   Never**

9. An old rule at school states that
only kids in the higher grades are
allowed to work in the school store.
You think this rule is ridiculous, and
you organize a petition so that all kids
can have a chance.   **Always   Sometimes   Never**

Do you stand up for what you believe in, even if it might prove difficult?
Or do you choose to take the simpler route and leave things as they are?
Add up your **Always**, **Sometimes**, and **Never** answers. Write the numbers below.

Always:_____   Sometimes:_____   Never:_____

Now read about your scores!

CHECK YOUR SCORE!

If you circled mostly Always: You have very strong opinions and convictions. You tend to argue your case and fight for what you believe in, even if your opinion is unpopular. Sometimes, though, you tend to argue an issue just for the sake of arguing! It is good to stand up for your beliefs, but you need to choose your battles wisely, so you'll win those battles that are most important to you.

If you circled mostly Sometimes: You tend to think through your convictions and opinions before acting on them. You might decide that some battles are worth fighting, while others are not. It is good to choose your battles wisely; just make sure the battles you choose are the right ones for you. Try not to let others talk you out of fighting for what you strongly believe in, even if that belief is not popular.

If you circled mostly Never: You tend to take the easy way out. Although you probably have strong beliefs or convictions, you are afraid to voice them. At times you might suggest an unpopular idea, but in the end, you go along with what others think or feel. You need to have more confidence in yourself and in your beliefs. Try to take a firm stand on one issue that you feel strongly about.

Activity #2

What does your child feel strongly about? Which convictions would he take a stand on? Invite him to write one conviction in the flow chart below and then describe what he could do to make others feel strongly about the issue, too. Ask him to complete the flowchart by explaining what happens next and describing the outcome. You might make extra copies of the flowchart, encouraging your child to record other moments when he takes a stand.

**MY CONVICTION
OR BELIEF**

HOW I CAN GET
OTHERS TO SEE
MY POINT OF VIEW

WHAT HAPPENED NEXT?

WHAT WAS THE OUTCOME?

RULE #50

Teach your child to be positive and enjoy life. Some things just aren't worth getting upset over. Help him to keep everything in perspective and focus on the good in his life.

Activity #1

Does your child tend to think that "the glass is half empty" or "the glass is half full"? Encourage him to take this test to find out. Read the test to him, and write down the letters and points of his answers. Then add up the points and read the score with him. For fun, take the test yourself! Have your child read the test to you and record your answers. See which of you is able to maintain a more positive attitude when things go wrong.

▸ A student you dislike has been chosen as the star of the school play, a role that you had also tried out for, a role that you really wanted. You:

1. Congratulate the student and are happy with your role in the chorus. (3)
2. Congratulate the student, but decide that there is no way you can be in the play. (2)
3. Ignore the student, drop out of the chorus, and refuse to see the play when it opens. (1)

▸ A movie you really wanted to see is sold out. You:

1. Stomp your foot, complain how unfair it is, and skip the movies altogether. (1)

2. Decide to see another movie. (3)

3. Decide to do something else now and go to a later show. (2)

▸ At dinner, the restaurant has run out of the special of the day. It was the only choice you had made. You:

1. Acknowledge that these things happen and choose something else. (3)

2. Refuse to order anything else; your appetite has been spoiled. (1)

3. Ask the waiter to recommend something that is as good as the special. (2)

▸ Your science-fair project wins second place. You were hoping for first place. You:

1. Reevaluate your project and try to figure out why it isn't first-place material. (2)

2. Feel happy that you won a ribbon at all. (3)

3. Point out all the things wrong with the first-place winner and explain why your project was better. (1)

▸ Your class is reading a book that you absolutely don't like. You:

1. Read it, but refuse to learn anything from it. (1)

2. Read it, but point out how stupid it is to your classmates. (2)

3. Read it and try to understand what you are supposed to learn from it. (3)

▸ A clothing store does not have the pair of pants you like in your size. You:

1. Feel disappointed, but look for another style of pants. (3)

2. Feel disappointed and don't feel like shopping anymore. (1)

3. Feel disappointed and move on to another store. (2)

► You try out for the basketball team and make the junior squad or the second string. You:

1. Accept your position, but complain about it to your friends. (2)
2. Accept the coach's decision and are happy to be chosen at all. (3)
3. Decide not to play until you can be on the "real" team. (1)

► You don't have the courage to invite someone to the school dance. Instead, you:

1. Go to the movies with a group of friends and talk about how stupid the dance is. (2)
2. Stay home and feel sorry for yourself. (1)
3. Go to the dance with a group of friends and have a great time. (3)

► On your way to a concert, the car breaks down. You:

1. Throw a tantrum about how much you really wanted to go to the concert. (1)
2. View the breakdown as an adventure and something funny to tell your friends. (3)
3. Remain calm and wait for the car to be fixed or wait for another ride. (2)

► You've volunteered to make dinner, but you need an ingredient that is not in the kitchen. You don't have a ride, so you can't go to the store. You:

1. Try to be creative and make something else or something new. (3)
2. Make the same dish anyway and explain why it might not taste good. (2)
3. Explain that you were not able to make dinner because you didn't have all the ingredients. (1)

If you scored 25–30: You're an optimist! You never let circumstances beyond your control bring you down or get in your way. You see the bright side of everything, and consequently, you are generally a happy person. Your positive attitude is contagious. Keep it up!

If you scored 18–24: You can find the silver lining! You are able to see the silver lining in most situations. Sometimes you let disappointments get you down, but for the most part, you learn to work with what you've got—or with what you've been given—and you try to have fun, despite not getting what you want. Good for you!

If you scored 11–17: Oh, woe is me! You tend to let things get you down when they shouldn't. Sometimes you are able to find the upside of a down moment, but usually you feel sorry for yourself. You need to say good-bye to this self-pity party and learn to be more positive. Try it—you'll like it!

If you scored 1–10: What a pessimist! You let every little disappointment ruin your life. In the process, you ruin the good times, good moods, and good feelings of others. Instead of always seeing how terrible everything is, try to imagine that things could be worse. Strive for more positive and happy feelings, and the people and circumstances around you will be happier, too.

Activity #2

What should we say when things go wrong? Read the phrases in the speech balloons with your child. Draw an X through the speech balloons that we should *not* say because they sound negative and make us feel bad. On the next page, write the things we *should* say because they sound positive and make us feel better.

Now write the positive phrases from the speech balloons in this Smiley Face chart!
Add a few positive phrases of your own to the chart, too.

☺

1. _____

2. _____

3. _____

4. _____

5. _____

6. _____

7. _____

8. _____

9. _____

10. _____

11. _____

12. _____

13. _____

14. _____

15. _____

RULE #51

Teach your child to live so that she will never have regrets. If there is something she wants to do, she should *do it!* She should never let fear, doubt, or other obstacles stand in her way. If there is something she wants, she should fight for it with all of her heart. If there is something she wants to be, she should do whatever is necessary in order to live out that dream.

Activity #1

Oftentimes the thing that holds us back from what we really want to do is fear. Although it is hard to recognize and acknowledge these fears, being able to conquer our fears and get past them is the best way to move forward and achieve what we really want out of life. Read about the people below with your child. Have her write down the fear that the person needs to overcome to achieve his or her goal. Talk about the fears your child recognizes, and gently discuss if she has similar fears.

1. Marcus wanted desperately to visit Africa, yet he'd always been afraid to fly. When his school decided to send a group of exchange students for study in Africa, Marcus considered going, but then he decided not to, even though it was a dream trip.

What was Marcus afraid of? _____

_____

2. More than anything, Cara loved to sing. She had joined the school choir, and she felt comfortable singing within a large group of people. The choir director was holding auditions for soloists for the holiday show. Cara wanted to audition, but she was afraid she wasn't good enough. What if the other kids laughed at her? Cara decided that being in the chorus was a safer choice.

What was Cara afraid of? _____

_____

3. Davis loved watching stand-up comedians, and it was his dream to be a stand-up comedian one day. There was only one problem—Davis had stage fright. He broke out in a sweat and started to shake when he had to give a report in class. A local restaurant was having an "open mike" night for performers. Davis really wanted to try it, but in the end he chickened out.

What was Davis afraid of? _____

_____

4. Shauna wanted to try out for the swim team. She loved swimming at the community pool during the summer, and she thought it would be fun to compete. But what if she didn't make it? What if she wasn't good enough? Then she'd always feel like a loser. Shauna decided it was better to swim by herself than to be part of a team.

What was Shauna afraid of? _____

_____

5. Calvin's teachers thought Calvin would excel in advanced math classes. They wanted him to take a special placement test. His parents were very proud, and Calvin wanted the challenge. But then he thought about it. He'd always done badly on standardized tests. What if he did poorly this time? Then everyone would be disappointed in him. Calvin decided it was best to stay in the regular math class.

What was Calvin afraid of? _____

_____

6. A new restaurant was opening in Jada's neighborhood, and she really wanted to be a waitress there. The day the restaurant began accepting applications, Jada arrived early. However, the restaurant was already packed with kids trying to get a job there. Jada figured she'd never have a chance against so many applicants, so she went home.

What was Jada afraid of? _____

_____

Activity #2

Encourage your child to think of some things that he would really like to do. It could be goals for his future as an adult or a more immediate school or personal goal. Have him write the goals below, list any fears that might hold him back, and describe the best and worst things that could happen. Suggest strategies that can help him overcome these fears.

WHAT I'D REALLY LIKE TO DO

1. _____

2. _____

3. _____

4. _____

5. _____

WHAT MIGHT HOLD ME BACK (MY FEARS)

_____

_____

_____

_____

_____

WHAT'S THE WORST THING THAT COULD HAPPEN?

1. _____

2. _____

3. _____

4. _____

5. _____

WHAT'S THE BEST THING THAT COULD HAPPEN?

_____

_____

_____

_____

_____

RULE #52

Your child should accept that he is going to make mistakes. Help him learn from them and move on.

Activity #1

Does your child tend to blow mistakes out of proportion, or is he able to acknowledge mistakes and move on? Invite him to take this test to find out. Have him circle the number that best describes how he reacts to each situation, as described below. You might make a copy of the quiz and take it yourself to compare your results with his.

0: You deny that it's your fault.

1: You acknowledge your mistake and then move on.

2: You acknowledge your mistake and try to figure out what you could have done differently.

3: You acknowledge your mistake and let it bother you for days.

1. You do poorly on a test that you studied hard for. How do you react?   0   1   2   3

2. You gossip about a friend, and she overhears you. How do you react?   0   1   2   3

3. You forget your homework assignment, and the class is denied an after-lunch snack. How do you react?

0   1   2   3

4. You oversleep and miss the bus, so your mother has to drive you to school. How do you react?

0   1   2   3

5. You burn the toast at breakfast and don't have time to make new toast. How do you react?

0   1   2   3

6. You spill water all over your group's science project, and the charts have to be rewritten. How do you react?

0   1   2   3

7. You realize that you called a new classmate by the wrong name. How do you react?

0   1   2   3

8. You go grocery shopping for your family, only to remember that you forgot to buy cat food for the cat. How do you react?

0   1   2   3

9. You forget to have an adult sign your permission slip for a class field trip. How do you react?

0   1   2   3

10. You accidentally knock over an expensive vase at someone's home and it breaks. How do you react?

0   1   2   3

If you scored 25–30: You need to chill out! You overreact all the time, no matter how big or small the mistake. You will make mistakes—everyone does! You need to learn how to control your emotions, accept responsibility for your mistakes, and move on.

If you scored 18–24: You tend to be even-tempered, but you also tend to blame yourself when things go wrong. You need to accept that mistakes happen. You acknowledge your mistakes and try to fix them, but sometimes to a fault. It's good to try to fix a mistake—if it's fixable. If not, let it go.

If you scored 11–17: You don't usually let mistakes affect you. You are aware enough to know when you've made a mistake, and you try to learn from it, but you don't let that one mistake rule your life and your decisions afterward. You take the lesson for what it's worth and then continue on. You should probably spend a little bit more time analyzing your mistakes, but in all, you have a healthy reaction to how you handle your slipups.

If you scored 0–10: You need to warm up! You never admit when you've made a mistake, choosing instead to pretend that the mistake didn't happen. Although that might make you feel better, you will never learn if you don't accept that you can and will make mistakes. You also tend to blame circumstances for the mistakes you make instead of taking the blame yourself. Nobody likes to be wrong, but then again, nobody likes to be around others who feel they are always right, either. Step up to the plate and acknowledge your mistakes!

Activity #2

Invite your child to discuss a mistake she made in the past that upset her. Ask her what she learned from the situation. What would she do differently next time? How would behaving differently have changed the outcome? Reassure her that learning from mistakes is the first step to correcting them. Make sure she understands that you have confidence in her ability to make good decisions in the future.

RULE #53

No matter what the circumstances, children and adults should always be honest. If your child has done something wrong in school, she should admit it to the teacher, who will respect her honesty and perhaps forgo any disciplinary measures.

Activity #1

The letters below have been written to an advice columnist named Honestly Truthful. Read each letter with your child. Then work with her to solve the problem, relying on honesty and truthfulness to guide your advice.

Dear Honestly Truthful,

I must be the worst person on the planet. I was laughing and talking in class one day when we had a substitute teacher. The teacher kept telling my friends and me to be quiet, but we didn't listen. Somehow, the substitute got our names wrong, and now the wrong people are being blamed. When those who were falsely accused pointed their fingers at my friends and me, we denied that we were to blame. Now I feel awful! What should I do?

Signed,
Giggled and Guilty

Dear Guilty,

_____

_____

_____

_____

Dear Honestly Truthful,

Okay, I know I'm going to sound like a coward, but I couldn't help it! I had a huge test for geography, but instead of studying for it, I decided to hang out at the mall with my friends. As if that wasn't bad enough, the morning of the test, I pretended to be sick. I lied to my mom and told her I had a stomachache. Now my stomach hurts more than ever! What should I do?

Signed,
Cheesy Queasy

Dear Queasy,

_____

_____

_____

_____

Dear Honestly Truthful,

I told the biggest lie to my grandparents. They wanted me to come over last weekend to see their pictures from their vacation to Antarctica, but I wanted to go to the school football game with my friends. I didn't want to hurt their feelings by telling them I had other plans, so instead I said I had a huge project I had to work on for school. Now I feel really guilty, and I feel that I have hurt them more by lying to them. What should I do?

Signed,
Football Fiasco

Dear Fiasco,

_____

_____

_____

_____

Activity #2

Challenge your child to unlock the Square of Truth on page 223 to reveal the secret message about telling the truth. Then discuss with him what the saying means and how he should apply the message to his own life.

THE SQUARE OF TRUTH!

To unlock the message of the square, count the squares in threes and circle the third letter. Write the letter on the line. The first one has been done for you. Keep going!

1	2	3	1	2	3
Y	T	(H)	T	P	O
Y					H
S					O
T					N
C					E
E	S	I	B	E	L

H __ __ __ __ __ __ is always

__ __ __ __ __ __

__ __ __ __ __ __ !

RULE #54

Carpe diem. Help your child realize that he only lives today once, so he mustn't waste it. Life is made up of special moments, many of which happen when people take action and seize the day.

Activity #1

Is your child more likely to seize the day or shy away? Encourage him to take this test to see if he is a "seize-er" or a "shy-er." Have him check the answer that best tells what he would do in each situation below. You might want to take the test, too, and compare your responses with his.

1. Your teacher asks you to speak to a lower grade, sharing your expert knowledge on a favorite topic or hobby. You . . .
_____ can't wait to get started.   _____ politely decline. How scary would *that* be?

2. Your friends are all going on the new roller coaster at the amusement park. Roller coasters scare you, but you are curious. You . . .
_____ hop on and let loose.   _____ wait for them until the ride is over.

3. Your favorite restaurant has a new menu. You . . .

_____ try a new entrée.   _____ look for your favorite dish.

4. Your music teacher suggests that you try out for the school musical. You . . .

_____ jump at the opportunity and   _____ shake your head and say you're
find a song for the audition.   not good enough.

5. Instead of working with your best friend on your social studies project, you find yourself paired with someone you hardly know. You . . .

_____ take the opportunity to get   _____ grumble to yourself that your
to know your new partner   project would be better if you
better.   could work with your friend.

WHAT KIND OF PERSON ARE YOU?

If you checked mostly answers on the left side: You are always up for new challenges, and you enjoy the opportunity to try new experiences. To you, life is one big adventure, and you can't wait to see what opportunities will come up next.

If you checked mostly answers on the right side: You tend to shy away from new experiences, and you often feel intimidated by the things you don't know or that are unfamiliar to you. You can change, though! The next time you're offered a chance to try something new, seize the day! Instead of thinking of the negatives or what could go wrong, think of the positives or what could go right!

If you checked half and half: You don't mind trying new things, but you are also very comfortable with the old tried and true. And there's nothing wrong with that! Working with people we know or eating foods we like makes us happy. Every once in a while, though, try to step outside your comfort zone and give something new a try. You never know—you might enjoy it!

Activity #2

What does carpe diem mean to your child? Encourage her to fill in the acrostic below with phrases that express the idea of carpe diem in her own words. Each phrase should start with a letter in the words carpe diem. The phrases can refer to new experiences she would like to try or ways that she interprets the concept of carpe diem. Explain that there is no right or wrong answer. You simply want your child to *seize the opportunity* to be thoughtful and let ideas flow.

CARPE DIEM—WHAT DOES IT MEAN?

C _____

A _____

R _____

P _____

E _____

D _____

I _____

E _____

M _____

Seize the Day!

RULE #55

Teach your child to be the best person she can be.

Activity #1

To be the best person we can be, we should have seven things in our lives: laughter, family, adventure, good food, challenge, change, and the quest for knowledge. Encourage your child to list examples of each of these seven items that help her make her life complete. Tell her to review the list if she ever feels down or uninspired.

What things make you **laugh**?

1. _____   2. _____

3. _____   4. _____

Who in your **family** helps you when things get tough?

1. _____   2. _____

3. _____   4. _____

What **adventures** do you recall that you really enjoyed?

1. _____   2. _____

3. _____   4. _____

What are some of your favorite **foods** that make you happy?

1. _____   2. _____

3. _____   4. _____

What things **challenge** you, either at home, at school, or in your personal life?

1. _____   2. _____

3. _____   4. _____

What **changes** can you think of that made your life richer or fuller?

1. _____   2. _____

3. _____   4. _____

In your **quest for knowledge,** what would you like to learn about, explore, or do?

1. _____   2. _____

3. _____   4. _____

Activity #2

Your child deserves an award for being the best that he can be! Invite him to complete the medal below. In the ribbons, have him list the things about himself that he is proud of—accomplishments at school, positive personality traits, special talents, and so on. Make sure you tell him that you are proud of him, too!

This medal is
awarded to

_____

for these outstanding
accomplishments!

Ron Clark takes America to School.

In his new book, Ron Clark introduces 11 key themes that will inspire teachers, parents and children, in the classroom and beyond.

Get excited about school with lessons and inspiration on 11 themes, including:

- **ADVENTURE** — How to make true educational excursions—not just field trips.

- **REFLECTION** — Activities that make learning meaningful and memorable.

- **HUMOR** — How to laugh and learn at the same time.

- **ENTHUSIASM** — Making education fun!

- **APPRECIATION** — Teaching children, parents, peers, and administration how to show appreciation for each other.

Author of the *New York Times* Bestseller *The Essential 55*

Ron Clark

THE EXCELLENT 11
ISBN: 1-4013-0141-X

"Mr. Clark gave me the strength to hold on and be somebody. He is the one who believed in me."

—Tamara, sixth-grade student, Harlem, New York

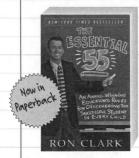

Now in Paperback

The *New York Times* bestseller that's become a must-read for parents and teachers—now in paperback.

THE ESSENTIAL 55
ISBN: 0-7868-8816-4

Put *The Essential 55* rules into practice—with fun activities and exercises to fire up children's imaginations.

THE ESSENTIAL 55 WORKBOOK
ISBN: 1-4013-0770-1

A teacher since 1995, Ron Clark has taught in some of the most challenging schools in the country. Since winning the **2001 Disney Teacher of the Year Award**, Clark has spoken to teachers, PTAs, and school boards across the country.

ALSO AVAILABLE ON
HYPERION
AUDIOBOOKS

HYPERION

Ron Clark...changing America, one child at a time.